PAT BROWN, MBA

# FootballMoney101

*Using Football to Teach the Basics of Money*

ABRAM · 47 · BROWN

*First published by AbramBrown47 2026*



*First edition*

*ISBN: 978-1-967737-50-5*

*This book was professionally typeset on Reedsy.*
*Find out more at reedsy.com*

# Contents


*Foreword* v
*Introduction* vii
*About This Book* ix
*Foolish Assumptions* xi
*How This Playbook Is Organized* xiii
*About Pat Brown* xv
Part I: Building the Foundation (The Preseason) 1
Chapter 1: Why Money Feels Complicated After Football 3
Chapter 2: Know the Scoreboard: Your Financial Snapshot 8
Chapter 3: Game Planning Your Money: Budgeting and Saving 13
Chapter 4: Credit, Debt, and Playing With Borrowed Money 18
Chapter 5: The Locker Room of Money: Banking Basics 23
Part II: Defense Wins Championships (Protection and Risk) 29
Chapter 6: Risk Tolerance and Risk Capacity: Know Your... 31
Chapter 7: Insurance Fundamentals Every Player Needs 37
Chapter 8: Life, Disability, and Liability Coverage 43
Part III: Offense and Execution (Investing Fundamentals) 49
Chapter 9: What Investing Really Is and How the Market Game... 51
Chapter 10: Risk, Reward, and the Power of Compounding 57
Chapter 11: Stocks Without the Hype 63
Chapter 12: Bonds and Playing Defense in Your Portfolio 69
Chapter 13: Funds, ETFs, and Team-Based Investing 75
Chapter 14: Real Estate and Alternative Plays 82
Part IV: Managing the Season (Portfolio Management) 89
Chapter 15: Asset Allocation: Building the Right Lineup 91
Chapter 16: Buying, Holding, and Staying Disciplined 99

Chapter 17: Rebalancing and Halftime Adjustments 107
Chapter 18: The Mental Game of Money 115
Part V: The Long Game (Taxes, Family, and Life Stages) 124
Chapter 19: Taxes and Where to Hold Your Money 126
Chapter 20: Retirement Accounts and Financial Independence 134
Chapter 21: Housing and Big Financial Decisions 142
Chapter 22: Your Career Is Your Greatest Asset 150
Chapter 23: Estate Planning Basics for Every Player 159
Chapter 24: Talking About Money With Family 168
Part VI: Staying in the Game Long-Term 177
Chapter 25: Advisors, Scams, and Winning Over the Long Haul 179
Chapter 26: Losing the Schedule and Rebuilding Structure 183
Chapter 27: From Teammates to Coworkers 187
Chapter 28: When No One Is Watching Anymore 191
Chapter 29: Redefining Winning After the Uniform Comes Off 196
Chapter 30: Staying Connected Without Living in the Past 202
*Glossary of Football and Financial Terms* 208
*Disclaimers* 214

# Foreword

Every football player understands this truth early.

Talent opens the door, but discipline keeps you in the building.

For years, athletes have been coached on how to train their bodies, study film, execute under pressure, and compete at a high level. They are taught how to prepare for opponents, adjust mid-game, and handle adversity when things do not go their way.

What they are rarely taught is how to manage money with the same discipline.

Too many athletes leave the game with memories, injuries, and pride but without a plan. Some never make significant money and still struggle because no one showed them how to manage what they had. Others earn more than they ever imagined and lose it just as quickly because opportunity arrived before education.

This book exists because that gap is real.

Football teaches habits that translate directly to financial success. Accountability. Preparation. Consistency. Patience. Long-term thinking. The problem is not that athletes lack the mindset. The problem is that no one ever connected the dots.

Football Money 101 does exactly that.

This is not a book about getting rich quick. It is not about stock tips, hype, or shortcuts. It is about building a foundation the same way you built yourself as a player. One rep at a time. One season at a time. One smart decision stacked on top of another.

The lessons in these pages are simple, but they are not easy. Just like football, success comes from doing the basics well over and over again. From avoiding unforced errors. From staying disciplined when emotions run high. From trusting the process even when progress feels slow.

If you approach your finances the same way you approached your sport, you give yourself an advantage most people never have. You already know how to work. You already know how to commit. You already know how to respond to coaching.

This book is your financial playbook.

Read it the way you would study film. Apply it the way you would execute a game plan. Respect the fundamentals, and do not skip steps.

Football may end.

The habits you build here do not have to.

Winning after the whistle is possible.

# Introduction

The final whistle is different than people think.

It is not loud.

It is not dramatic.

It does not feel like an ending.

Most of the time, it feels quiet.

One day you are on a schedule. Lifts, meetings, film, practice, games. Someone tells you where to be, when to be there, and what is expected of you. There is a depth chart. A playbook. A standard. Accountability is built into the system.

Then one day, it stops.

No meetings.

No structured offseason.

No coach checking effort.

No locker room.

And suddenly, everything that used to be managed for you is now on you. Your time. Your money. Your decisions. Your future.

This is where a lot of athletes get caught off guard.

Not because they are lazy.

Not because they are reckless.

Not because they lack intelligence.

But because there is no playbook after the final whistle.

Nobody hands you a guide on how to manage a paycheck. Nobody explains taxes before your first real income. Nobody walks you through budgeting, credit, insurance, investing, or long-term planning in a way that makes sense to someone who thinks in reps, seasons, and game plans.

So athletes do what athletes always do. They rely on instinct. They listen to the loudest voice in the room. They chase momentum. They trust people who sound confident. They make decisions under pressure without a system.

That works in football.

It does not work with money.

Football is a game of structure. Money without structure turns into chaos.

This book exists to fix that problem.

Football Money 101 is not about turning you into a finance expert. It is about translating what you already know how to do into a new arena. You already understand preparation. You already understand discipline. You already understand that effort is non-negotiable and shortcuts get exposed.

Those same principles apply to money.

If you can follow a strength program, you can follow a budget.

If you can study film, you can review your finances.

If you can trust a game plan, you can trust a long-term investment strategy.

If you can make adjustments at halftime, you can adjust when life changes.

This book will meet you where you are.

Whether you are a current athlete, a former athlete, or someone who still thinks like one, the goal is the same. Build a foundation. Avoid the big mistakes. Learn how to protect what you earn. Put yourself in position to win long after the uniform comes off.

There will be no hype in these pages. No shortcuts. No promises of overnight success. Just fundamentals, discipline, and a clear plan you can execute.

Football ends.

Life does not.

You may not have been given a playbook after the final whistle, but you have one now.

Let's get to work.

# About This Book

This book is not meant to be read like a textbook.

It is meant to be used like a playbook.

Football players learn differently than most people. You learn through reps, film, correction, and accountability. You understand systems. You understand roles. You understand that success comes from doing the basics well and doing them consistently.

That is exactly how this book is designed.

Every concept in Football Money 101 is taught using football thinking. Not metaphors for the sake of creativity, but real parallels that make sense if you have ever sat in a locker room, watched film, or been held accountable by a coach.

Money works a lot like football.

There is preparation before the season starts.

There is execution during the game.

There are adjustments when things do not go as planned.

And there are consequences when fundamentals are ignored.

This book will show you how to approach money the same way you approached football. With a plan. With discipline. With patience. And with long-term vision.

You do not need a finance background to understand this material. You do not need to memorize formulas or learn complicated terminology. If you understand effort, reps, assignments, and accountability, you already have what you need.

Each chapter follows a consistent structure.

It starts with a football scenario you will recognize immediately. A moment under pressure. A decision point. A situation where discipline matters.

From there, the financial concept is explained by mapping it directly to how football works. Nothing abstract. Nothing theoretical.

You will also hear from the coach's perspective throughout the book. Not in a literal sense, but in the way coaches reinforce habits. Clear expectations. Honest feedback. No shortcuts.

At the end of each chapter, you will find a short section called Athlete Takeaways. These are not summaries. They are reminders. Simple, coachable points you can apply immediately.

You do not need to read this book straight through if you do not want to. Just like a playbook, some sections will matter more to you right now than others. But if you do read it from start to finish, the progression is intentional. Foundations first. Protection next. Execution after that. Then long-term planning.

This book will not promise you financial success. Football never promised wins either. What it will give you is a system. A framework. A way to think about money that matches how you already think about competition and preparation.

Winning with money does not require talent.

It requires discipline.

You already have that.

This book shows you how to use it.

# Foolish Assumptions

Every good playbook starts with assumptions.

Not because the coach thinks every player is the same, but because a system only works when everyone understands the baseline. This book is no different.

In true Football Money 101 fashion, these assumptions are called "foolish" not because they are wrong, but because they are honest. They may not apply perfectly to everyone, but they apply well enough to build something that works.

Here is what this book assumes about you.

It assumes you understand discipline.

You have shown up early. You have stayed late. You have done workouts when no one was watching. You know the difference between talent and effort, and you know that effort is non-negotiable.

It assumes you have been coached hard.

You have been corrected. You have been held accountable. You have heard things you did not want to hear and learned to respond instead of react. You understand that feedback is not personal. It is part of improvement.

It assumes you understand preparation.

You know that games are not won on Saturday. They are won on Monday, Tuesday, and Wednesday in practice and film. You understand that consistency beats intensity.

It assumes you are competitive.

You care about outcomes. You want to improve. You want to win. Even if you are no longer playing, that edge is still there.

It assumes you are not a financial expert.

You may know some things. You may have picked up bits and pieces along the way. But no one handed you a clear, structured financial education designed for how you think and learn. That is not a failure. That is reality.

It assumes you have made mistakes or will make some along the way.

Every athlete has blown an assignment. Every athlete has learned the hard way. Money is no different. This book assumes you are willing to learn, adjust, and keep moving forward.

It assumes you are willing to take responsibility.

Not for everything that has happened to you, but for what happens next. Football teaches ownership. This book expects the same.

It also assumes you want something more than short-term wins.

You want stability. You want options. You want to protect yourself and the people you care about. You want to build something that lasts beyond one season or one paycheck.

If these assumptions feel fair, this book will work for you.

If you are looking for shortcuts, guarantees, or someone else to blame, this is not the right playbook.

Football rewards those who do the work.

Money works the same way.

These assumptions are the foundation.

Everything else builds from here.

# How This Playbook Is Organized

This book is organized the same way a football season is.

You do not start with trick plays.

You do not skip conditioning.

You do not worry about the scoreboard before you know the assignments.

Everything builds in the right order.

Football Money 101 is broken into six parts, each one designed to mirror how football actually works and how money decisions unfold over time.

**Part I: Building the Foundation (The Preseason)**

This is where everything starts. Conditioning. Fundamentals. Discipline. You learn how money flows in and out of your life, how to manage cash, credit, and basic systems, and how to avoid the early mistakes that derail seasons before they start. Nothing flashy. Just the work that makes everything else possible.

**Part II: Defense Wins Championships (Protection and Risk)**

Before you worry about scoring, you have to protect yourself. This section focuses on risk, insurance, and decision-making under pressure. In football, bad defense loses games. In money, poor protection can wipe out years of effort. This part teaches you how to stay in the game.

**Part III: Offense and Execution (Investing Fundamentals)**

This is where you move the ball. Investing, compounding, and long-term strategy are introduced using football concepts you already understand. The focus is not on big plays, but on consistent execution. You learn how to score without abandoning discipline.

**Part IV: Managing the Season (Portfolio Management)**

No season goes exactly as planned. Injuries happen. Roles change. Life does the same thing to your finances. This section teaches you how to review, adjust, and stay disciplined over time without overreacting or panicking.

**Part V: The Long Game (Taxes, Family, and Life Stages)**

Football ends. Life does not. This part addresses the realities that show up after the uniform comes off. Taxes, retirement, housing, careers, and family conversations all live here. These are the decisions that determine long-term outcomes.

**Part VI: Staying in the Game Long-Term**

The final section focuses on leadership and accountability. Knowing when to ask for help. How to work with advisors. How to avoid scams. How to learn from mistakes and stay focused on winning over decades, not just one season.

Each chapter follows the same structure so you know what to expect. A football scenario. A clear financial lesson. A coach's perspective. Real decision points. And a short set of Athlete Takeaways you can apply immediately.

You can read this book cover to cover, or you can jump to the sections that matter most right now. Just like a playbook, not every page is needed in every moment.

But the order matters if you want the full benefit.

Start with the foundation.

Protect what you earn.

Execute with discipline.

Adjust when necessary.

Think long term.

That is how football works.

That is how money works.

This playbook shows you how to connect the two.

# About Pat Brown

Pat Brown played college football at the University of Kansas from 1994 to 1999 and was named team captain for the 1999 season. His years in the locker room shaped his views on accountability, discipline, preparation, and leadership, principles that continue to guide his work long after football.

Following his playing career, Pat transitioned into financial services and built a career as a financial advisor and wealth manager. He works with individuals, families, business owners, and athletes navigating increasingly complex financial lives. He pursued advanced education and professional development, earning an MBA along with industry designations including ChFC®, RICP®, and CAP®. His background blends academic training with real-world experience in financial planning, retirement income strategies, tax planning, and philanthropy.

As the college sports landscape changed with the introduction of Name, Image, and Likeness opportunities, Pat recognized a growing education gap. Student athletes were gaining access to income, contracts, and endorsements without the financial knowledge needed to manage taxes, cash flow, business structures, and long-term consequences. That reality became the catalyst for his work in the NIL space.

Pat has since become a recognized voice in athlete financial education and has been interviewed by national publications and platforms including Financial Planning, Yahoo, and ESPN Andscape, where he shares insights on NIL planning, financial literacy gaps, and the challenges facing student athletes and their families.

These experiences led Pat to author a series of practical, athlete-focused books designed to meet athletes and families where they are. His NIL-related titles include *Financial Literacy for NIL*, *Financial Literacy for NIL for Parents of Student Athletes, Financial Literacy for NIL for High School Students,* and *Financial Literacy for NIL for International Student Athletes.* Each book is written to be clear, accessible, and grounded in real-world scenarios rather than theory.

Pat also created a growing collection of sport-specific financial education titles, including *Football Money 101, Baseball Money 101, Basketball Money 101, Cheer Money 101, Dance Money 101, Gymnastics Money 101, Hockey Money 101, Lacrosse Money 101, Rowing Money 101, Soccer Money 101, Softball Money 101, Tennis Money 101, Track Money 101, Volleyball Money 101,* and *Wrestling Money 101.* Each book translates the culture, discipline, and mindset of the sport into financial lessons athletes can apply long after competition ends.

To extend this mission beyond books, Pat founded Former Student Athlete, a platform created to support athletes navigating life after sports. Former Student Athlete provides education, community, and real-world resources focused on financial literacy, career transitions, health, identity, and long-term success once the uniform comes off. His broader education platforms can be found at www.formerstudentathlete.com, www.financialliteracyfornil.com, www.financialliteracyforstudentathletes.com, and www.parentsofstudentathletes.com.

Pat is easy to find through a Google search, on LinkedIn, or on Twitter, where he regularly shares insights on athletes, money, and life after sports. If you would like to visit with Pat specifically about *Football Money 101,* you can reach him directly at info@footballmoney101.com.

Pat's work is rooted in a belief shaped by both football and finance. Athletes deserve a better playbook for life after sports, and financial education should arrive before opportunity turns into regret.

# Part I: Building the Foundation (The Preseason)

**You cannot win games without conditioning, fundamentals, and discipline.**

Every football season starts the same way.

Before the lights, before the crowd, before the scoreboard matters, there is preseason.

Preseason is not glamorous. There are no highlights. No applause. No shortcuts. It is conditioning. Fundamentals. Reps. Accountability. It is learning how to show up every day and do the work when nobody is watching.

Money works the exact same way.

Most financial mistakes athletes make do not come from bad intentions or lack of intelligence. They come from skipping the preseason. From trying to play games without conditioning. From wanting results before building a foundation.

You would never expect to step on the field without knowing the playbook.

You would never expect to win without understanding assignments.

You would never expect success without discipline.

Yet that is exactly how many athletes are forced to approach money.

This section of the book is about building your financial foundation the same way you built your football foundation. We start with awareness. We build discipline. We focus on fundamentals before strategy. We learn how to control what we can control.

Before you invest.

Before you take risks.

Before you chase opportunities.

You need to understand how money flows in and out of your life. You need to know your numbers. You need to learn how to manage cash, credit, and basic systems that support everything else.

Preseason is where habits are formed.

Preseason is where discipline is tested.

Preseason is where championships are actually built.

If you get this part right, everything that follows becomes easier.

If you skip it, you will spend your financial life playing catch-up.

This is the work.

This is the foundation.

This is where winning starts.

# Chapter 1: Why Money Feels Complicated After Football

Think back to your first day of fall camp.

You did not walk in expecting to run the entire playbook. You focused on alignment. Assignments. Footwork. Getting through practice without blowing something simple. Coaches did not care about flash. They cared about fundamentals.

Money rarely starts that way.

Most athletes are thrown into financial decisions without a camp, without a depth chart, and without a coach. One day you are managing a stipend or small paycheck. The next day you are dealing with real income, contracts, taxes, and expectations. No walkthroughs. No preseason.

And when mistakes happen, they do not get corrected in the film room. They show up on bank statements, credit reports, and tax notices.

That is why money feels complicated. Not because it actually is, but because nobody ever taught it the way athletes learn.

## *Why Personal Finance Is Rarely Taught to Athletes*

Athletes grow up in structured systems. Your job is to train, compete, and perform. Someone else handles the schedule, the meals, the equipment, and often the paperwork. That structure is not a bad thing. It is what allows you to focus.

The problem is what happens when the structure disappears.

Schools assume money education is someone else's responsibility. Teams assume athletes will figure it out later. Families often assume income equals understanding. By the time real money shows up, education is already late.

Football teaches you how to prepare for opponents. It rarely teaches you how to prepare for a paycheck.

So when money enters the picture, athletes do what they always do. They rely on instincts, confidence, and the advice of people around them. That works on the field. With money, it leads to mistakes.

## *Locker Room Money Myths That Lead to Mistakes*

Every locker room has money talk.

Someone knows a guy who made a killing in crypto. Someone else claims investing is gambling. Someone swears debt is always bad or always fine. The loudest voice often sounds the most confident.

Common myths sound like this:

If you are not investing, you are falling behind.

If you are investing, you should be aggressive.

Debt is either poison or free money.

Saving is for people who do not make enough.

These myths spread because they are simple and emotional. They are also wrong.

Football does not work on myths. You would never change your technique because someone said it worked for them once. Money should be treated the same way.

## *Saving vs Investing vs Gambling*

This confusion causes more damage than almost anything else.

Saving is about protection. It is cash you can access quickly. Emergency funds. Short term needs. Stability.

Investing is about ownership and growth over time. It requires patience. Volatility is normal. Results come from staying in the system.

Gambling is chasing outcomes without a plan. No protection. No margin for error. Emotion driven decisions.

In football terms, saving is conditioning. Investing is running the offense. Gambling is forcing throws into double coverage and hoping it works.

Athletes often skip saving because it feels slow. They jump straight to investing or worse, speculation. That is like skipping warmups and expecting to play four quarters at full speed.

## *Why Starting Simple Beats Waiting for Perfect*

One of the biggest mistakes athletes make with money is waiting.

Waiting until they make more.

Waiting until they understand everything.

Waiting until the timing feels right.

Football does not reward waiting. Reps matter. Early mistakes are how you learn.

Money works the same way.

You do not need the perfect budget. You need a basic one.

You do not need the perfect investment strategy. You need consistency.

You do not need to know everything. You need to start.

Starting simple builds confidence. Confidence builds discipline. Discipline builds results.

The athlete who wins long term is not the one who tries to make the biggest play. It is the one who stays in position, executes the plan, and stacks good days.

## *Coach's Perspective*

If your coach were talking about money, it would sound familiar.

Effort is non-negotiable.

Do your job.

Make the simple play.

Control what you can control.

We do not take plays off.

Money does not need heroics. It needs discipline. Coaches preach fundamentals because fundamentals hold up under pressure. Money is no different.

### *Game Situations and Decision Points*

You get your first real paycheck. Do you spend first and hope there is something left, or do you set aside money before anything else?

You hear about a hot investment. Do you chase it without understanding, or stick to a plan you can execute?

You realize you have no emergency fund. Do you ignore it and hope nothing happens, or start building protection now?

These decisions mirror football moments. Force the play, or take what the defense gives you.

### *Common Athlete Mistakes and Financial Parallels*

Athletes get impatient.

Financially, that looks like chasing quick wins.

Athletes trust confidence over preparation.

Financially, that looks like following bad advice.

Athletes hate feeling behind.

Financially, that leads to reckless decisions.

The same mistakes that lose games lose money.

### *Winning the Long Game*

Football careers are short. Financial lives are long.

You do not need to win today. You need to stay in the game. The goal is not perfection. It is progress. The athletes who win with money are the ones who treat it like a season, not a single drive.

## *Athlete Takeaways*

- Do not skip the preseason. Fundamentals come before flash.
- Saving is protection. Investing is execution. Gambling is guessing.
- Loud locker room advice is not a game plan.
- Simple and consistent beats perfect and delayed.
- Stay disciplined and stack good days.

# Chapter 2: Know the Scoreboard: Your Financial Snapshot

Every Monday starts the same way.

You walk into the meeting room, sit down, and the film comes on. The scoreboard is right there. No opinions. No excuses. Just the result.

You might feel like you played well. You might remember one big hit, one clean block, one drive where everything clicked. But the film does not care how you feel. It shows every missed assignment, every blown block, every detail you wish you could forget.

That is why film matters.

Football does not reward confidence without execution. It rewards awareness. Teams that win consistently know exactly where they stand, even when it is uncomfortable.

Money works the same way.

Money has a scoreboard too. Most athletes avoid it. Not because they are irresponsible, but because nobody ever taught them how to read it. Bank balances, credit cards, loans, subscriptions, and random spending feel scattered and overwhelming. So instead of reviewing the film, they rely on gut feel.

"I think I'm doing okay."

"I make decent money."

"I'll look at it later."

That is how small mistakes turn into big problems.

Before you can fix anything, before you can improve, before you can feel confident about your future, you need to know the score.

## *Income, Expenses, and Cash Flow*

Cash flow is how money moves through your life.

Income is what comes in.

Paychecks. NIL income. Bonuses. Side work. Business income.

Expenses are what go out.

Rent. Food. Travel. Training. Lifestyle. Bills you notice and bills you do not.

Cash flow is the difference between the two.

In football terms, income is yards gained. Expenses are yards allowed. Cash flow determines whether you are moving the ball forward or backing yourself up.

A lot of athletes focus only on income. More money feels like progress. A raise. A contract. A check. It feels like momentum.

But if expenses rise at the same speed, nothing actually improves.

You can make six figures and still live paycheck to paycheck. You can earn more and feel more stressed at the same time. That usually means cash flow is broken.

Positive cash flow gives you options.

Negative cash flow puts you under pressure.

Pressure changes decision-making. When you are always backed up near your own goal line, you force throws. You rush plays. You take risks you would not take if you had room to operate.

Money works the same way.

You do not need complicated spreadsheets to start. You need awareness. Know what comes in. Know what goes out. Everything else builds from there.

## *Assets, Liabilities, and Net Worth*

Assets are things you own that have value.

Cash. Investments. Property. Businesses. Retirement accounts.

Liabilities are what you owe.

Credit cards. Student loans. Car loans. Personal loans. Mortgages.

Net worth is the difference between the two.

In football terms, assets are your strengths. Liabilities are vulnerabilities. Net worth is the overall matchup.

One big asset does not erase multiple liabilities. Just like one star player does not fix a broken unit. You have to look at the whole picture.

Many athletes confuse income with wealth. Income is what you earn. Net worth is what you keep and build over time.

A high-income athlete with high debt is not ahead.

A lower-income athlete with discipline and growing assets may be winning quietly.

Net worth is the long-term scoreboard. It tells you whether you are building something sustainable or just surviving season to season.

## *Fixed vs Variable Expenses*

Not all expenses are created equal.

Fixed expenses stay mostly the same.

Rent. Insurance. Loan payments. Subscriptions you forgot you had.

Variable expenses change.

Food. Travel. Entertainment. Shopping. Convenience spending.

Fixed expenses are like your base defense. They define your structure. Variable expenses are your play calls. That is where adjustments happen.

Athletes often focus on cutting big things they cannot easily change. Rent. Car payments. Insurance. Those matter, but they are harder to adjust quickly.

The real leverage is usually in variable spending you do not notice.

Small leaks sink ships.

Daily coffee. Late-night food. Ride shares. Streaming services. "It's only twenty dollars" adds up faster than you think.

Winning teams fix details. Not just big plays.

### *Film Study on Where Your Money Actually Goes*

This is the hardest part, and the most important.

Pull the statements. Bank accounts. Credit cards. Loans. Look at the transactions.

No judgment. No excuses. Just facts.

Film study is not about punishment. It is about improvement.

You might be surprised. Small purchases add up. Subscriptions you forgot about keep charging. Convenience costs more than you think. Patterns show up quickly once you look.

This is where most people quit. They feel uncomfortable. They feel exposed. So they stop looking.

But you cannot fix what you do not see.

Film tells the truth.

### *Coach's Perspective*

A coach would not let you guess your performance.

The film does not lie.

Know the score.

Details matter.

If you do not look at it, you cannot fix it.

Avoiding the scoreboard does not change it. Reviewing it gives you control.

### *Game Situations and Decision Points*

You feel like you are doing fine, but your account balance never grows. Do you blame income, or review expenses?

You get a raise. Do you let lifestyle rise with it, or improve cash flow?

You have debt but no clear picture of what you owe. Do you ignore it, or list it out and face it?

Same situation as football. Watch the film or repeat the mistake.

### *Common Athlete Mistakes and Financial Parallels*

Athletes rely on feel instead of film.

Financially, that means guessing instead of tracking.

Athletes avoid bad tape.

Financially, that means avoiding statements.

Athletes overestimate one good play.

Financially, that means one big paycheck masking poor habits.

### *Winning the Long Game*

Great teams know the score at all times. Not just at the end of the game.

Knowing your financial snapshot is not about judgment. It is about awareness. Awareness leads to control. Control leads to confidence.

This is how you stop playing from behind.

### *Athlete Takeaways*

Know the score before you change the game plan.

Income means nothing without positive cash flow.

Assets build strength. Liabilities create pressure.

Fixed expenses define structure. Variable expenses offer adjustment.

Watch the film. The truth sets you up to win.

# Chapter 3: Game Planning Your Money: Budgeting and Saving

Before every game, there is a plan.

Not a hope.

Not a vibe.

A plan.

You know the opponent. You know your strengths. You know what you are trying to do on the first drive and what adjustments are ready if things go sideways. Nobody walks into a game saying, "Let's just see what happens."

Money is no different.

Yet this is where many athletes change behavior. They train with structure. They lift with structure. They watch film with structure. But when it comes to money, they freestyle. Spend first. React later. Hope it works out.

That is not a game plan. That is playing defense all the time.

Budgeting and saving are how you run the offense in your financial life. They give you control, pace, and options. Without them, you are reacting to pressure instead of dictating outcomes.

## *Budgeting Systems That Actually Work*

A budget is not punishment.

It is not restriction.

It is not telling yourself "no" all the time.

It is not a moral judgment on your spending.

A budget is a game plan.

In football terms, a budget is knowing where the ball is supposed to go. It assigns roles. It sets expectations. It keeps you from forcing plays when the situation does not call for it.

Good budgeting systems share three traits.

They are simple.

They are realistic.

They are repeatable.

If a system is too complicated, it will break under pressure. Coaches do not install playbooks players cannot execute on third down with the crowd loud and the clock running. Your budget should work the same way.

At its core, a budget answers three questions.

How much comes in?

What has to go out?

What is left to deploy?

That is it.

You do not need to track every penny perfectly. You need clarity. Awareness beats precision when precision leads to burnout.

When you know your numbers, decisions get easier. You stop guessing. You stop reacting emotionally. You stop being surprised by outcomes that were actually predictable.

That is running the offense.

## *Automating Savings Like Practice Reps*

Nobody debates whether to show up to practice.

It is automatic. Built into the schedule. You do not wake up and ask yourself if you feel like lifting today. You just go.

Saving should work the same way.

If you wait to save what is left over, you will rarely save anything. Life fills the space. Convenience wins. Discipline fades.

Automation fixes that.

Direct deposit into savings.

Automatic transfers on payday.

Retirement contributions taken before money hits your account.

No decision required.

In football terms, this is scheduled reps. You do not negotiate with the weight room. You do not debate conditioning. You trust the process and show up.

Automation removes emotion. Emotion is where mistakes live.

When savings happens automatically, progress becomes boring and boring is good. Boring means consistent. Consistent means effective.

## *Emergency Funds as Injury Insurance*

Every player understands injury risk.

You do not plan to get hurt. You prepare for it anyway.

An emergency fund is the financial version of that mindset.

It is cash set aside for unexpected events. Medical bills. Car repairs. Job changes. Delayed paychecks. Family emergencies. Life happening when it does not ask permission.

Without an emergency fund, every surprise becomes a crisis. You reach for credit. You panic. You abandon the plan you worked hard to build.

With an emergency fund, you stay composed. You handle the situation. You protect momentum.

That is staying in the game.

Emergency funds are not about earning returns. They are about buying stability. Stability allows you to keep making good decisions under pressure.

That matters more than interest.

## *Balancing Lifestyle Today With Wins Tomorrow*

This is where many athletes struggle.

You work hard. You sacrifice. You push your body and your time. Wanting to enjoy the moment is valid.

The mistake is turning short-term rewards into long-term damage.

Football teaches delayed gratification. You train now so you can perform later. You watch film now so mistakes do not repeat on Saturday. Money requires the same discipline.

You do not have to live like a monk. You do have to choose intentionally.

Spend on what matters to you.

Cut what does not.

Protect future options.

Lifestyle upgrades are not the enemy. Unplanned lifestyle creep is.

Winning tomorrow starts with discipline today.

## *Coach's Perspective*

A coach would say it plainly.

Do your job.

Be consistent.

Details win games.

Do not cheat the work.

Trust the process.

Budgets and savings are boring for the same reason conditioning is boring.

They work.

## *Game Situations and Decision Points*

You get paid. Do you save first or hope there is something left?

You want a lifestyle upgrade. Do you check the budget or ignore the plan?

An unexpected expense hits. Do you stay calm or reach for credit?

Just like football, the situation matters less than the response.

Execution defines outcomes.

### *Common Athlete Mistakes and Financial Parallels*

Athletes skip conditioning.

Financially, that looks like skipping savings.

Athletes overestimate what they can handle.

Financially, that leads to no emergency fund.

Athletes reward effort with shortcuts.

Financially, that shows up as lifestyle creep.

### *Winning the Long Game*

You cannot win without a plan.

Budgeting and saving are not about control. They are about freedom.

Freedom to make choices instead of reacting.

Freedom to handle adversity without panic.

Freedom to stay aggressive when opportunities show up.

Running the offense means setting the tempo instead of playing catch-up.

### *Athlete Takeaways*

A budget is a game plan, not a restriction.

Save first, not what is left. Make it automatic.

Emergency funds keep you calm under pressure.

Lifestyle choices today affect options tomorrow.

Discipline off the field wins games later.

# Chapter 4: Credit, Debt, and Playing With Borrowed Money

Every coach has said it at some point.

"Do not put the team in a bad spot."

That warning usually shows up around penalties, missed assignments, or forcing plays that were never there. One mistake can flip momentum. One bad decision can change field position. Sometimes it changes the entire game.

Borrowed money works the same way.

Debt gives you leverage, but it also magnifies mistakes. It can help you move the ball when used with discipline, or it can back you up fast when used carelessly.

Debt is not automatically bad. It is borrowed money. And borrowed money always comes with expectations.

If you use it the right way, it can help you move the chains.

If you misuse it, it puts you behind them.

## *How Credit Scores and Reports Really Work*

Your credit score is not a moral judgment.

It is not a reflection of your intelligence, your work ethic, or your character. It is a report card on how you handle borrowed money.

Credit scoring systems look at patterns of behavior, not intentions. They focus on questions like:

Do you pay on time?

How much of your available credit do you use?

How long have you been using credit?

Do you apply for new credit frequently?

Do you carry balances or pay them down?

In football terms, credit is trust.

When a coach trusts you, you stay on the field. You get responsibility. You get opportunities. When you miss assignments, that trust erodes quickly.

Your credit report is the film. It shows every snap. Every missed block. Every late payment. Your credit score is the grade.

You cannot argue with it. You cannot explain it away. You can only improve it through consistent behavior.

That is good news. Trust is earned through repetition.

## *Credit Cards, Loans, and Interest*

Credit cards and loans are tools.

Like any tool, they can help or hurt depending on how you use them. A hammer can build a house or break a window. Credit works the same way.

Interest is the cost of borrowing.

It is the defense charging you yardage every time you hold the ball. The longer you keep the ball, the more yardage you give up.

Carry balances too long and interest compounds against you. That is like playing uphill football. You can still move the ball, but it takes more effort, more plays, and leaves less margin for error.

Minimum payments are especially dangerous. They make debt feel manageable while quietly stretching the game against you. Progress slows. Fatigue sets in. Options disappear.

Used correctly, credit can smooth cash flow and build trust. Used poorly, it becomes a trap that limits flexibility and forces rushed decisions.

## *Good Debt vs Bad Debt*

Not all debt is created equal.

Good debt helps you build something that lasts. Education that increases earning potential. A business that generates income. A reasonably priced home that provides stability.

Bad debt finances consumption. Lifestyle. Status. Short-term pleasure with long-term cost.

In football terms, good debt is investing in training and development. You put in the work now so performance improves later.

Bad debt is skipping practice to look good on game day. The appearance improves briefly, but fundamentals suffer and mistakes show up under pressure.

The difference is not just the interest rate. It is what the debt produces.

Does it create opportunity?

Does it improve long-term position?

Does it increase options or restrict them?

That is the real test.

## *Debt Traps That Sideline Careers*

Most debt problems do not start with disaster. They start with comfort.

The biggest traps are simple.

Using credit to fund lifestyle.

Ignoring balances because payments feel manageable.

Co-signing without understanding the risk.

Assuming income will always cover mistakes.

Athletes often feel invincible early. Winning streaks create confidence. So does steady income.

But debt does not care how hard you work. It cares how consistent you are.

Co-signing is one of the most dangerous traps. When you co-sign, you are not helping someone else borrow money. You are borrowing it yourself.

If they miss a payment, the hit shows up on your film.

That is not loyalty. That is risk without control.

## *Why Debt Feels Easy at First*

Debt feels helpful in the beginning.

It solves problems quickly. It removes friction. It allows upgrades without waiting. That ease is why it is dangerous.

In football terms, this is forcing early throws because they worked once. Eventually, defenses adjust.

Debt always adjusts.

Interest compounds. Payments stack. Flexibility shrinks. The game gets harder the longer you play it this way.

Discipline early keeps you from needing discipline later under pressure.

## *Coach's Perspective*

A coach would not sugarcoat it.

Value the ball.

Do not beat yourself.

Know the situation.

Protect field position.

One bad decision can change the game.

Debt magnifies decisions. Handle it with respect.

## *Game Situations and Decision Points*

You can put it on a card. Do you do it because it is convenient, or because it fits the plan?

You qualify for a loan. Do you ask if you should take it, or just if you can?

Someone asks you to co-sign. Do you understand the risk, or feel pressured?

These are fourth-down decisions. Think before you snap the ball.

### *Common Athlete Mistakes and Financial Parallels*

Athletes chase comfort early.

Financially, that shows up as lifestyle debt.

Athletes trust momentum too much.

Financially, that leads to over-borrowing.

Athletes ignore small mistakes.

Financially, that becomes long-term damage.

### *Winning the Long Game*

Borrowed money can help you build or break you.

The difference is discipline.

Play within your system. Protect field position. Avoid unnecessary risks.

Use debt intentionally or do not use it at all.

The best teams win because they do not beat themselves.

### *Athlete Takeaways*

Credit is trust. Protect it.

Interest is the defense. Do not let it win.

Borrow to build, not to impress.

Manage debt before it manages you.

One bad decision can change the season.

# Chapter 5: The Locker Room of Money: Banking Basics

Every team has a locker room.

It is not glamorous. No fans see it. No highlights come from it. But everything depends on it. That is where gear is stored. Meetings happen. Preparation begins. If the locker room is disorganized, nothing else runs smoothly. Equipment gets lost. Time gets wasted. Focus disappears.

Your banking system is the locker room of your money.

Most athletes never think about it. They open accounts wherever is convenient, swipe their card, and move on. But when the system is sloppy, money leaks out quietly. Fees add up. Payments get mistimed. Fraud slips through. Stress increases.

Before you worry about investing, building wealth, or long-term growth, your locker room has to function.

If the foundation is messy, everything built on top of it suffers.

## *Checking vs Savings Accounts*

Checking accounts are for movement.

Savings accounts are for storage.

Checking is where money flows in and out. Paychecks. Bills. Groceries. Gas. Daily spending. It is active and constantly changing.

Savings is where money sits with purpose. Emergency funds. Short-term goals. Protection against surprises. It is meant to be boring and untouched most of the time.

In football terms, checking is the field. Savings is the sideline.

You need both.

If everything is on the field all the time, you are exposed. One hit, one mistake, one bad bounce and the ball is loose. If everything is on the sideline, you are not playing the game.

Problems start when athletes blur the two.

When savings is treated like spending money, discipline disappears. When checking holds too much, temptation increases. When everything lives in one account, awareness drops.

Separation creates clarity. Clarity creates control.

## *Why Separation Matters More Than People Think*

Most financial stress comes from poor separation.

Bills hit unexpectedly. Balances feel confusing. You are never sure how much is actually safe to spend. That uncertainty creates hesitation and bad decisions.

In football terms, this is not knowing who is responsible for which assignment. Confusion leads to blown coverage.

Clear roles prevent mistakes.

Checking handles operations. Savings handles protection. Mixing the two creates chaos.

## *Online Banks vs Traditional Banks*

Traditional banks offer branches, tellers, and face-to-face access. Online banks typically offer lower fees, better interest rates, and convenience.

There is no universal right answer.

The right choice is the one that fits your system.

Some athletes like being able to walk into a branch and talk to someone. Others prefer efficiency, mobile access, and fewer fees. Both are valid.

In football terms, this is scheme fit.

Some players thrive in spread offenses. Others perform better in power systems. The goal is not copying someone else's setup. The goal is choosing what works for you and running it consistently.

What matters most is not the logo on the building. It is understanding how your bank operates, what it charges, and how quickly it moves money.

## *How Money Actually Moves*

Money does not teleport.

It moves through systems.

Direct deposit.

Electronic transfers.

Debit cards.

Automatic payments.

Pending transactions.

Most financial problems are timing problems, not income problems.

A paycheck posts later than expected. A bill hits earlier than planned. A transfer takes longer than you assumed. Suddenly you are overdrawn even though you technically have money.

In football terms, this is a timing route thrown too early or too late. The idea was right. The execution was off.

Knowing when money leaves and when it arrives matters. Knowing processing times matters. Knowing cutoff times matters.

Awareness prevents penalties.

## *Overdrafts Are Preventable Mistakes*

Overdrafts are rarely about emergencies.

They usually come from ignoring timing.

Automatic payments hitting without a buffer. Transfers taking longer than expected. Spending right up to zero.

In football terms, this is lining up offsides. It is avoidable if you pay attention.

Keeping a buffer in checking solves most overdraft issues. Separating savings prevents accidental transfers. Alerts provide early warnings.

You would not ignore the play clock. Do not ignore account timing.

## *Protecting Yourself From Fraud and Mistakes*

Fraud does not require negligence. It requires opportunity.

Loose systems create opportunity.

Protect yourself by doing the basics consistently.

Monitor accounts regularly.

Set transaction alerts.

Use strong passwords.

Keep savings separate.

Act immediately when something looks wrong.

In football terms, this is assignment discipline.

Teams that miss assignments get exposed. Systems without oversight get exploited.

Fraud is easier to fix when caught early. Delays increase damage and stress.

## *Why Banking Feels Boring but Matters*

Banking is boring.

There are no highlights. No excitement. No immediate reward.

That is exactly why it matters.

The boring parts of football are what allow the exciting parts to work. Alignment. Communication. Fundamentals. Conditioning.

Banking is foundational. When it works, you do not notice it. When it fails, everything else suffers.

## *Coach's Perspective*

A coach would keep it simple.

Protect the locker room.

Details matter.

Do not create your own problems.

Handle your business.

No coach tolerates sloppy preparation. Banking is preparation.

## *Game Situations and Decision Points*

You use one account for everything. Do you separate systems or keep guessing?

You get hit with a fee. Do you fix the system or ignore it?

You notice a suspicious charge. Do you act immediately or hope it resolves itself?

These are small moments that define long-term outcomes.

Championships are lost through small mistakes repeated often.

## *Common Athlete Mistakes and Financial Parallels*

Athletes ignore details.

Financially, that means fees and errors.

Athletes trust systems blindly.

Financially, that means missed issues.

Athletes avoid boring work.

Financially, that leads to chaos.

## *Winning the Long Game*

A clean locker room supports everything else.

Good banking does not make headlines. It does not create bragging rights. It quietly keeps you organized, protected, and ready.

When your banking system works, saving becomes easier. Investing becomes smoother. Stress decreases. Confidence increases.

Control starts with organization.

## *Athlete Takeaways*

Checking is for movement. Savings is for protection.

Choose banks that fit your system, not someone else's.

Know how and when your money moves.

Protect against fraud the same way you protect the ball.

Clean systems keep you in control.

# Part II: Defense Wins Championships (Protection and Risk)

**If you cannot protect what you earn, nothing else matters.**

Every championship team has one thing in common.

They protect the ball.

They protect the quarterback.

They protect the lead.

Offense gets the attention, but defense is what keeps you in games long enough to win them.

Money works the same way.

You can earn well. You can invest smart. You can have momentum. None of it matters if one bad event, one lawsuit, one injury, or one reckless decision wipes it out.

Most athletes focus on earning first. That makes sense. Football rewards production. But smart teams also know that protection is not optional. It is built into the system.

This section of the book is about defense.

Defense is not fear.

Defense is not playing small.

Defense is playing smart.

It is understanding risk before it shows up. It is knowing what could hurt you and putting protection in place ahead of time. It is staying in position so one bad play does not turn into a touchdown.

Risk is not just about investments. It shows up in health, liability, contracts, income, and life events you cannot control. Ignoring it does not make it go away. Preparing for it keeps you in the game.

Great defenses are disciplined. They communicate. They know their assignments. They do not chase every play. They force the offense to earn everything.

That is exactly how you should approach money.

In this section, you will learn how to identify risk, understand your limits, and protect what you have worked for. You will learn how insurance actually works, where it helps, and where athletes commonly get it wrong.

This is not about eliminating risk. Football is a contact sport. Life has contact too.

This is about managing risk so one hit does not end your season.

If you skip defense, you are betting everything on perfection.

Perfection does not exist.

Championships are won by teams that can score and protect.

This is how you protect your future.

# Chapter 6: Risk Tolerance and Risk Capacity: Know Your Limits

Every coach knows this moment.

You are down late. The crowd is loud. Momentum is swinging. Someone on the sideline yells for a big play. Maybe a trick play. Maybe a deep shot. Something aggressive.

But the coach pauses.

Not because they are scared.

Because they know the team.

They know who can execute under pressure. They know who is banged up. They know the situation, the clock, the field position, and the risk of failure.

That is not playing conservative.

That is coaching reality.

Money decisions work the same way.

Risk is not about what sounds exciting. It is about what fits your real situation.

## *Emotional Risk vs Financial Risk*

Most people talk about risk tolerance. How much risk you feel comfortable taking.

That matters, but it is not the whole picture.

Risk capacity is more important. Risk capacity is how much risk you can actually handle without breaking your system.

Athletes often confuse the two.

Emotionally, you may feel comfortable taking risks. You have competed your whole life. You are used to pressure. You trust yourself to respond when things go wrong. You believe you can recover from mistakes.

Financially, that may not be true.

If one bad outcome would force you into debt, require you to sell investments at the wrong time, or derail your life plans, then your risk capacity is lower than your confidence suggests.

In football terms, this is knowing the difference between wanting the ball and being the right option in that moment.

Confidence matters. Context matters more.

Great players understand that not every situation calls for heroics. Sometimes the smartest play is the one that keeps the game under control.

### *Why Confidence Can Be Misleading*

Athletes are trained to believe in themselves. That mindset is necessary to compete at a high level. But in money decisions, confidence without structure can be dangerous.

Financial markets, income, and life events do not respond to effort the way sports do. You cannot outwork a market downturn. You cannot grind your way out of a liquidity problem overnight.

Risk capacity is about margin.

How much room do you have for error?

How much time do you have to recover?

How many things have to go right for this decision to work?

Ignoring those questions does not make you bold. It makes you exposed.

## *Time Horizon and Flexibility*

Time horizon matters more than people realize.

If you need money soon, you cannot afford big swings. Volatility becomes risk because there is no time to recover.

If money is for decades from now, short-term swings matter less. Time absorbs mistakes.

Flexibility is the hidden variable.

Can you adjust if things go wrong?

Do you have savings?

Stable income?

Support systems?

The ability to reduce expenses temporarily?

A team with depth can take more chances. A team dealing with injuries and fatigue cannot.

Money works the same way.

Two people can make the same decision and experience completely different outcomes because their flexibility is different.

Risk should always be evaluated alongside time and flexibility, not in isolation.

## *How Risk Impacts Every Decision*

Risk is not just about investing.

It affects how much cash you keep.

How much debt you take on.

What type of insurance you need.

How aggressive your lifestyle choices are.

How quickly you lock yourself into long-term commitments.

Every decision carries downside. Ignoring that downside does not remove it.

In football terms, every play has a worst-case outcome. Coaches still call plays, but they understand the risk before the ball is snapped.

Money decisions deserve the same awareness.

Before making a choice, ask one simple question.

What happens if this does not go my way?

If the answer includes panic, forced selling, or long-term damage, the risk may not fit your situation.

## *Matching Risk to Real Life*

Smart teams match strategy to personnel.

Smart athletes match financial risk to real life.

If your income is unstable, you need more protection.

If you have dependents, you need more margin.

If you are early in your career, you need flexibility.

If your timeline is short, you need stability.

There is no universal right level of risk.

There is only what fits your situation right now.

Trying to copy someone else's risk is like running someone else's playbook. It fails fast because it ignores your strengths, weaknesses, and context.

Your risk strategy should evolve as your life evolves. What made sense at twenty-two may not make sense at thirty-two.

Adjustment is not weakness. It is awareness.

## *Coach's Perspective*

A coach would say it straight.

Know the situation.

Do not put the team in a bad spot.

Be smart, not reckless.

Control what you can control.

Risk is part of the game. Poor awareness is optional.

### *Game Situations and Decision Points*

You hear about an aggressive investment. Do you ask if it fits your timeline, or just if it has upside?

You consider a big purchase. Do you evaluate flexibility if income changes?

You want to take more risk because you feel confident. Do you check the downside first?

These are situational football decisions.

Awareness matters.

### *Common Athlete Mistakes and Financial Parallels*

Athletes trust confidence over context.

Financially, that leads to overexposure.

Athletes ignore fatigue and injuries.

Financially, that leads to ignoring limits.

Athletes chase momentum.

Financially, that leads to risk mismatches.

### *Winning the Long Game*

Risk is unavoidable. Failure is not.

The athletes who win long-term understand their limits and respect them. They take risks when it makes sense. They protect themselves when it does not.

They do not confuse aggression with intelligence.

That is not fear.

That is discipline.

Winning seasons are built on awareness, not impulse.

## *Athlete Takeaways*

Confidence does not equal capacity. Know the difference.

Time horizon determines how much risk you can take.

Flexibility gives you options under pressure.

Every decision has downside. Acknowledge it.

Smart risk keeps you in the game.

# Chapter 7: Insurance Fundamentals Every Player Needs

Every player understands this reality.

You can do everything right and still get hurt.

You can train hard, prepare correctly, follow the game plan, and execute at a high level, and one awkward step or one bad collision can change everything. Injuries do not ask permission. They do not care how disciplined you are or how much potential you have.

That is why teams invest so heavily in trainers, medical staff, equipment, and depth. They do not assume injuries will not happen. They assume contact is part of the game and prepare accordingly.

Insurance plays that same role in your financial life.

You do not buy insurance because you expect something bad to happen. You buy it because you understand that life has contact. Accidents, illnesses, and unexpected events are not failures. They are part of the environment.

Ignoring that reality does not make you tough. It makes you exposed.

## *Why Insurance Is About Availability*

In football, the most valuable trait is availability.

Talent does not matter if you cannot suit up. Potential means nothing if one hit sidelines you for the season.

Financially, availability works the same way.

If one unexpected event wipes out your savings, forces you into debt, or derails your progress, you were not protected. Insurance exists to keep you available to keep playing the long game.

It is not about fear.

It is about staying in position.

### *Health Insurance Basics*

Health insurance is non-negotiable.

It covers doctor visits, prescriptions, emergencies, surgeries, and major medical events that can otherwise destroy your finances. Without it, one injury or illness can erase years of hard work in a matter of weeks.

Athletes often assume they are healthy and therefore safe. That mindset works until it does not.

In football terms, skipping health insurance is like playing without pads. You might feel faster. You might feel free. But when contact happens, the damage is real and immediate.

Health insurance is not just about emergencies. It is about access.

Access to preventative care.

Access to early treatment.

Access to recovery instead of avoidance.

Know your plan.

Know what it covers.

Know what it does not cover.

Know your deductible.

Know your out-of-pocket maximum.

Do not wait until something goes wrong to learn how your coverage works. That is like learning the playbook in the middle of the game.

### *Auto and Renters Insurance*

Auto insurance protects you, your vehicle, and everyone else involved in an accident. Renters insurance protects your personal property and provides liability coverage if something happens where you live.

Both are often underestimated.

Athletes focus on obvious costs. Rent. Car payments. Training expenses. Insurance feels like background noise because nothing bad is happening right now.

But accidents do not announce themselves.

Auto insurance is about more than your car. It is about protecting yourself from lawsuits, medical costs, and long-term financial damage.

Renters insurance is not just about stolen electronics. It covers liability. If someone is injured in your apartment, you could be responsible.

In football terms, auto and renters insurance protect field position. One mistake should not put you in a hole so deep that the game is over.

## *Homeowners Insurance*

If you own a home, homeowners insurance is essential.

It protects the structure, your belongings, and your liability exposure. It also covers things most people never think about until they happen.

Fires.

Storms.

Water damage.

Accidents.

Legal claims.

Owning property without insurance is like running a defense with no safeties. Everything looks fine until one play gets behind you.

Homeownership adds responsibility. Insurance is how you manage that responsibility without putting your entire financial future at risk.

## *Deductibles, Premiums, and Coverage Limits*

This is where confusion usually starts.

Premiums are what you pay to keep the policy active.

Deductibles are what you pay out of pocket before coverage kicks in.

Coverage limits are the maximum the policy will pay.

Higher deductibles usually mean lower premiums. Lower deductibles usually mean higher premiums. There is no free lunch.

The goal is not to eliminate cost. The goal is balance.

You want coverage you can afford to maintain.

You want deductibles you can handle without panic.

You want limits that actually protect you if something serious happens.

In football terms, this is load management. Too much weight increases injury risk. Too little preparation increases exposure.

Insurance is not about getting every dollar back. It is about preventing financial catastrophe.

### *Why Being Underinsured Is Worse Than Paying a Little More*

Many people choose the cheapest policy without understanding what they are giving up.

That is dangerous.

Saving a small amount on premiums can cost you massively when it matters most. Underinsurance feels smart until it fails under pressure.

In football terms, this is cutting corners on equipment to save money. It works until the first hard hit.

The goal is not minimal coverage. The goal is adequate protection.

### *Coach's Perspective*

A coach would not debate this.

Protect yourself.

Know your assignments.

Do not leave yourself exposed.

Stay available.

Insurance is availability.

If one hit takes you out financially, you were not protected.

### *Game Situations and Decision Points*

You are healthy and considering skipping coverage. Do you save money now or protect against the unknown?

You want the cheapest policy possible. Do you understand what it does not cover?

You assume nothing bad will happen. Are you prepared if it does?

These are risk decisions. Awareness matters.

### *Common Athlete Mistakes and Financial Parallels*

Athletes underestimate injury risk.

Financially, that means skipping coverage.

Athletes focus on cost instead of protection.

Financially, that leads to underinsuring.

Athletes ignore details.

Financially, that leads to surprises when it matters most.

### *Winning the Long Game*

Insurance does not win games.

It keeps you in them.

You cannot control everything that happens. You can control how prepared you are when it does.

That is defense.

Strong teams respect defense. Strong financial plans do too.

### *Athlete Takeaways*

Insurance is pads for your financial life. Wear them.

Health coverage is non-negotiable.

Auto, renters, and homeowners insurance protect field position.

Premiums and deductibles are trade-offs. Know yours.

Protect availability. You cannot win from the sideline.

# Chapter 8: Life, Disability, and Liability Coverage

Every player understands this reality.

You can do everything right and still get hurt.

You can train hard, prepare correctly, follow the game plan, and execute at a high level, and one awkward step or one bad collision can change everything. Injuries do not ask permission. They do not care how disciplined you are or how much potential you have. They show up when they show up.

That is why teams invest so heavily in trainers, medical staff, equipment, and depth. They do not assume injuries will not happen. They assume contact is part of the game and prepare accordingly. Preparation is not pessimism. It is professionalism.

Insurance plays that same role in your financial life.

You do not buy insurance because you expect something bad to happen. You buy it because you understand that life has contact. Accidents, illnesses, lawsuits, and unexpected events are not failures. They are part of the environment.

Ignoring that reality does not make you tough.

It makes you exposed.

## Why Insurance Is About Availability

In football, the most valuable trait is availability.

Talent does not matter if you cannot suit up. Potential means nothing if one hit sidelines you for the season. Coaches trust players who are prepared to stay on the field.

Financially, availability works the same way.

If one unexpected event wipes out your savings, forces you into debt, or derails your progress, you were not protected. Insurance exists to keep you available so you can keep playing the long game.

It is not about fear.

It is about staying in position.

Insurance allows you to absorb hits without abandoning your plan. It keeps one bad moment from becoming a career-changing setback.

## Health Insurance Basics

Health insurance is non-negotiable.

It covers doctor visits, prescriptions, emergencies, surgeries, and major medical events that can otherwise destroy your finances. Without it, one injury or illness can erase years of hard work in a matter of weeks.

Athletes often assume they are healthy and therefore safe. That mindset works until it does not. Health is not permanent. Neither is protection without insurance.

In football terms, skipping health insurance is like playing without pads. You might feel faster. You might feel free. But when contact happens, the damage is real and immediate.

Health insurance is not just about emergencies. It is about access.

Access to preventative care.

Access to early treatment.

Access to recovery instead of avoidance.

Without coverage, people delay care. Small problems become big ones. Pain turns into long-term damage. Financial stress compounds physical stress.

Know your plan.

Know what it covers.

Know what it does not cover.

Know your deductible.

Know your out-of-pocket maximum.

Do not wait until something goes wrong to learn how your coverage works. That is like learning the playbook in the middle of the game.

## Auto and Renters Insurance

Auto insurance protects you, your vehicle, and everyone else involved in an accident. Renters insurance protects your personal property and provides liability coverage if something happens where you live.

Both are often underestimated.

Athletes focus on obvious costs. Rent. Car payments. Training expenses. Insurance feels like background noise because nothing bad is happening right now.

But accidents do not announce themselves.

Auto insurance is about more than your car. It is about protecting yourself from lawsuits, medical costs, lost income, and long-term financial damage. One accident can involve multiple parties, injuries, and legal claims.

Renters insurance is not just about stolen electronics. It covers liability. If someone slips, gets hurt, or claims damages in your apartment, you could be responsible.

In football terms, auto and renters insurance protect field position. One mistake should not put you in a hole so deep that the game is over.

## Homeowners Insurance

If you own a home, homeowners insurance is essential.

It protects the structure, your belongings, and your liability exposure. It also covers things most people never think about until they happen.

Fires.

Storms.

Water damage.

Accidents.

Legal claims.

Owning property without insurance is like running a defense with no safeties. Everything looks fine until one play gets behind you.

Homeownership adds responsibility. Insurance is how you manage that responsibility without putting your entire financial future at risk.

It is not optional protection. It is baseline defense.

## Deductibles, Premiums, and Coverage Limits

This is where confusion usually starts.

Premiums are what you pay to keep the policy active.

Deductibles are what you pay out of pocket before coverage kicks in.

Coverage limits are the maximum the policy will pay.

Higher deductibles usually mean lower premiums. Lower deductibles usually mean higher premiums. There is no free lunch.

The goal is not to eliminate cost. The goal is balance.

You want coverage you can afford to maintain.

You want deductibles you can handle without panic.

You want limits that actually protect you if something serious happens.

In football terms, this is load management. Too much weight increases injury risk. Too little preparation increases exposure.

Insurance is not about getting every dollar back.

It is about preventing financial catastrophe.

## Why Being Underinsured Is Worse Than Paying a Little More

Many people choose the cheapest policy without understanding what they are giving up.

That is dangerous.

Saving a small amount on premiums can cost you massively when it matters most. Underinsurance feels smart until it fails under pressure.

In football terms, this is cutting corners on equipment to save money. It works until the first hard hit.

The goal is not minimal coverage.

The goal is adequate protection.

## Coach's Perspective

A coach would not debate this.

Protect yourself.

Know your assignments.

Do not leave yourself exposed.

Stay available.

Insurance is availability.

If one hit takes you out financially, you were not protected.

## Game Situations and Decision Points

You are healthy and considering skipping coverage. Do you save money now or protect against the unknown?

You want the cheapest policy possible. Do you understand what it does not cover?

You assume nothing bad will happen. Are you prepared if it does?

These are risk decisions. Awareness matters.

## Common Athlete Mistakes and Financial Parallels

Athletes underestimate injury risk.

Financially, that means skipping coverage.

Athletes focus on cost instead of protection.

Financially, that leads to underinsuring.

Athletes ignore details.

Financially, that leads to surprises when it matters most.

## Winning the Long Game

Insurance does not win games.

It keeps you in them.

You cannot control everything that happens. You can control how prepared you are when it does.

That is defense.

Strong teams respect defense. Strong financial plans do too.

## Athlete Takeaways

Insurance is pads for your financial life. Wear them.

Health coverage is non-negotiable.

Auto, renters, and homeowners insurance protect field position.

Premiums and deductibles are trade-offs. Know yours.

Protect availability. You cannot win from the sideline.

# Part III: Offense and Execution (Investing Fundamentals)

**This is where you move the ball down the field.**

Defense keeps you in the game.

Offense wins it.

Once your foundation is solid and your protection is in place, it is time to move the ball. This is the part of the playbook most athletes are excited about. Investing. Growth. Momentum. Scoring.

But good offenses do not chase highlights.

They execute.

Every great offense starts with fundamentals. Knowing the formation. Understanding assignments. Trusting the system. Taking what the defense gives you. Staying patient when drives take time.

Investing works the same way.

This section is not about trick plays or getting rich quick. It is about consistent execution. Understanding how markets actually work. Knowing the difference between volatility and loss. Letting time and discipline do the heavy lifting.

Most investing mistakes athletes make come from trying to score too fast. Forcing throws. Abandoning the run. Letting emotion override the game plan.

Smart offenses do the opposite.

They stay balanced.

They protect the ball.

They adjust when needed.

They trust the process.

In this section, you will learn how to approach investing the same way you approached offense on the field. With structure. With patience. With awareness of risk and reward.

You will learn what you are actually owning when you invest. How different positions in a portfolio work together. Why diversification matters. And why boring often wins.

This is where discipline shows up.

If you skipped the foundation or ignored protection, offense becomes reckless. If you do this part right, investing becomes a tool instead of a gamble.

Moving the ball is not about one big play.

It is about sustaining drives.

This section shows you how to do that.

# Chapter 9: What Investing Really Is and How the Market Game Works

Every player remembers the first time the game felt fast.

The ball snapped, everything moved at once, and for a moment it felt chaotic. Defensive linemen were in your face. Receivers were running full speed. Coaches were yelling. The crowd was loud. Your instincts told you to react immediately, even if you were not sure to what.

Then something changed.

After enough reps, film sessions, and real game experience, the speed slowed down. You started recognizing formations. You understood tendencies. You knew where help was coming from. You stopped reacting to movement and started anticipating it.

The market works the same way.

To people on the outside, it looks random. Numbers flashing across a screen. Prices jumping up and down. Headlines screaming urgency. Opinions everywhere. It feels chaotic, unpredictable, and intimidating.

But underneath the noise is a system.

And once you understand that system, the chaos starts to make sense.

## How Financial Markets Function

At its core, the financial market is simple.

It is a place where ownership and capital are exchanged.

Companies raise money to grow. They use that money to hire people, build products, expand operations, and compete. Investors provide that money in exchange for a share of ownership or a promise of repayment.

Prices move based on expectations about the future, not just what is happening today. Markets are forward-looking. They react to earnings expectations, economic data, innovation, competition, and confidence.

In football terms, the market is the league.

Teams compete. Some are rebuilding. Some are contenders. Some are poorly managed. Others are disciplined and well-coached. Standings change week to week, but the season keeps moving forward.

The league does not stop because one team struggles. The market does not stop because one company fails.

Markets are not designed to be comfortable.

They are designed to function.

Understanding that difference changes how you respond to volatility.

## Stocks, Bonds, and Ownership

Stocks represent ownership.

When you buy a stock, you are not buying a ticker symbol. You are buying a piece of a real business. That business employs people, sells products, competes in an industry, and tries to grow profits over time.

When the business does well, owners benefit.

When the business struggles, owners feel it.

Bonds are different.

Bonds are loans. You lend money to a company or government in exchange for regular interest payments and the promise that your money will be returned later. Less upside. More predictability.

In football terms, stocks are offense.

They generate points. They create explosive plays. They drive long-term growth.

Bonds are defense.

They control damage. They stabilize the game. They keep things from getting out of hand when momentum shifts.

You do not win championships with offense alone.

You do not build durable wealth with growth alone.

Ownership is the key word.

Investing is not betting on price movement. It is owning productive assets over time and letting them work for you.

## Market Cycles and Volatility

Markets move in cycles.

Expansion.

Slowdown.

Correction.

Recovery.

Repeat.

Volatility is movement, not failure.

Prices rising and falling does not mean the system is broken. It means expectations are adjusting. Big swings feel uncomfortable because humans prefer certainty. Markets do not offer it.

In football terms, this is momentum.

No team dominates every quarter. No offense scores on every drive. Games swing back and forth. Good teams expect that. Poor teams panic when it happens.

Athletes who panic during volatility make the same mistake as players who abandon the game plan after one bad series.

Volatility does not mean something is wrong.

It means the game is being played.

The mistake is confusing movement with danger.

## Why Markets Feel Emotional

Markets involve money.

Money represents effort, time, security, and identity. When prices move, emotions follow. Fear during downturns. Excitement during rallies. Regret after missed opportunities.

The problem is not emotion. The problem is acting on it.

In football, emotion fuels intensity, but execution still follows structure. You do not change assignments because you are angry. You do not abandon coverage because the crowd is loud.

Markets demand the same discipline.

When emotion replaces structure, mistakes multiply.

## Long-Term Strategy vs Highlight Plays

Highlight plays are exciting.

A deep ball. A trick play. A fourth-down gamble. They grab attention and feel rewarding when they work. They are also high risk and inconsistent.

Long-term investing is about sustained drives.

Five yards. Six yards. First down. Ball control. Time of possession. Avoiding turnovers.

In football terms, disciplined teams win by executing boring plays extremely well. They do not need constant heroics. They need consistency.

Chasing hot investments is like throwing into double coverage.

Sometimes it works.

Most of the time it does not.

When it fails, the damage is immediate.

Markets reward patience more than brilliance.

## Why Time Matters More Than Timing

Many investors wait.

They want the perfect entry point. The perfect moment. Confirmation that things feel safe. The problem is that markets do not announce when uncertainty is gone.

Time in the market matters more than timing the market.

In football terms, skipping reps because you are waiting to feel ready keeps you unprepared. Experience is built by participation, not perfection.

You do not need to predict every move.

You need to stay in the game.

## Coach's Perspective

A coach would keep it simple.

Trust the system.

Do your job.

Take what the defense gives you.

Protect the ball.

Stay disciplined.

Great coaches do not call a new play every snap. They trust preparation.

Investing rewards discipline, not bravado.

## Game Situations and Decision Points

The market drops sharply. Do you panic or stick to the plan?

You hear about a hot opportunity. Do you chase it or evaluate whether it fits?

You feel behind financially. Do you force plays or stay patient and consistent?

Same game. Same rules.

Your response determines the outcome.

## Common Athlete Mistakes and Financial Parallels

Athletes react emotionally.

Financially, that leads to panic selling.

Athletes chase big plays.

Financially, that leads to speculation.

Athletes abandon structure.

Financially, that leads to chaos.

Discipline solves all three.

## Winning the Long Game

Markets reward ownership, patience, and discipline.

You do not need to predict every headline. You do not need to win every quarter. You do not need to outsmart everyone else.

You need to stay invested, stay balanced, and stay disciplined.

That is how chaos turns into opportunity.

## Athlete Takeaways

Investing is ownership, not gambling.

Markets move in cycles. Volatility is normal.

Stocks and bonds play different roles.

Highlight plays are tempting. Discipline wins.

Stay patient and execute the plan.

# Chapter 10: Risk, Reward, and the Power of Compounding

Every strength coach preaches the same thing.

You do not get stronger from one workout.

You get stronger from thousands of reps over time.

Nobody walks into the weight room expecting results in a week. You show up. You lift with intention. You recover. You eat. You sleep. You repeat. Most days feel ordinary. Progress is slow. Sometimes it feels invisible.

Then one day, something changes.

Weights that once felt heavy move easily. Conditioning improves. Confidence rises. What looked like "nothing happening" suddenly shows results.

Compounding works the same way.

Most people miss it because they are looking for immediate feedback. Athletes understand this concept better than almost anyone. You already know that consistency beats intensity. You already know that skipping reps costs more than bad days.

Money follows the same rules.

## Risk and Return Tradeoffs

There is no reward without risk.

In football, throwing the ball downfield creates opportunity, but it also creates risk. A deep shot can change a game or turn into an interception.

Running the ball is safer, but it limits upside. Coaches balance these tradeoffs constantly based on score, clock, field position, and personnel.

Investing works the same way.

Higher potential returns usually come with higher risk. Lower risk investments usually provide more stability but slower growth. There is no strategy that gives maximum return with zero risk. Anyone promising that is lying or confused.

The mistake is thinking risk should be avoided entirely.

Risk is part of progress. The goal is not eliminating risk. The goal is choosing the right amount of risk for your situation.

In football terms, you do not call deep shots on every play. You mix concepts. You take shots when the situation is right. You protect the ball when it is not.

Smart investing is situational awareness applied over time.

## Volatility vs Permanent Loss

This is one of the most misunderstood concepts in investing.

Volatility is movement.

Permanent loss is damage.

Markets going up and down is normal. Prices fluctuate. Headlines exaggerate. Fear and excitement rotate. None of that automatically means something is broken.

Permanent loss happens when you make decisions that cannot recover. Panic selling. Overleveraging. Taking on more risk than you can survive. Abandoning the plan at the wrong time.

In football terms, volatility is giving up a first down.

It happens. You adjust. You line up and play the next snap.

Permanent loss is a turnover.

It changes momentum. It shortens the field. It creates damage that takes time to overcome.

Athletes often confuse discomfort with danger. Seeing red numbers feels bad, so they assume something is wrong. In reality, volatility is the price of growth. The danger comes from reacting emotionally instead of executing the plan.

## Why Athletes Are Actually Built for Compounding

Athletes train in systems that mirror compounding perfectly.

Strength gains stack. Conditioning builds. Technique sharpens. Mental toughness grows. None of it happens in isolation. Each rep builds on the last.

You do not reset to zero after a bad workout. You carry forward everything you have built.

Compounding is growth on top of growth.

Your money earns returns. Those returns earn returns. Over time, the effect accelerates. The early years look boring. The later years look powerful.

In football terms, this is stacking good days.

One good practice does not change a season.

A year of good practices does.

Time is the multiplier.

The earlier you start, the more powerful compounding becomes. Not because you are smarter. Because you gave the system more time to work.

## The Real Cost of Waiting

Waiting feels safe.

"I'll start when I make more money."

"I'll start when I understand it better."

"I'll start when the market feels stable."

Those thoughts feel responsible. They are not.

Every year you delay is a year compounding cannot work for you. That lost time cannot be recovered. You cannot cram years of compounding into the future.

In football terms, skipping offseason training puts you behind before camp even starts. You cannot catch up by working harder later. The foundation was never built.

You do not need to start big.

You need to start now.

Small contributions done consistently beat perfect plans done someday.

## Why Consistency Matters More Than Market Conditions

Many people believe compounding only works in "good markets."

That is false.

Compounding works because you keep showing up. Contributions made during downturns often matter more than contributions made during rallies. You buy more when prices are lower. You build position quietly.

In football terms, this is training during losing seasons. It does not feel rewarding. It is often overlooked. But it is what sets teams up for future success.

Consistency removes the need for prediction.

You do not need to know what the market will do next year. You need to know what you will do regardless.

## Coach's Perspective

A coach would say it plainly.

Reps matter.

Be consistent.

Trust the process.

Do not cheat the work.

No coach builds a program around motivation. Motivation fades. Systems hold.

Compounding rewards discipline the same way training does.

## Game Situations and Decision Points

The market drops sharply. Do you stop investing or keep showing up?

You feel behind financially. Do you force risk or stay disciplined?

You want to wait for the perfect moment. Do you start anyway?

Same decisions. Same principles.

The outcome depends on execution, not conditions.

## Common Athlete Mistakes and Financial Parallels

Athletes chase quick results.

Financially, that leads to over-risking.

Athletes skip recovery.

Financially, that leads to burnout and bad decisions.

Athletes delay preparation.

Financially, that leads to lost time and missed opportunity.

The pattern is always the same. Short-term thinking undermines long-term progress.

## Why Compounding Rewards Discipline, Not Talent

Some athletes are more talented than others.

Some investors are smarter than others.

Neither matters as much as consistency.

The athlete who trains year-round beats the one who relies on bursts of intensity. The investor who stays invested beats the one who jumps in and out based on feelings.

Compounding does not care how confident you are. It cares how consistent you are.

That is why it works so well for disciplined people and so poorly for emotional ones.

## Winning the Long Game

Compounding does not reward brilliance.

It rewards consistency.

Stay invested.

Stay patient.

Keep showing up.

Let time do what it does best.

The work always shows up eventually.

## Athlete Takeaways

Risk and reward are always connected.

Volatility is normal. Permanent loss is avoidable.

Compounding rewards consistency over time.

Waiting costs more than mistakes.

Start now and keep showing up.

# Chapter 11: Stocks Without the Hype

Every team has that moment on film.

A player tries to do too much. Instead of taking the easy gain, they bounce it outside, spin, reverse field, and turn a positive play into a loss. The crowd might have loved it if it worked, but the coach hates it because it breaks the system.

It was not a talent issue.

It was a discipline issue.

Stocks get treated the same way.

People chase the flashy play. The hot name. The big story. The promise of quick upside. They want the touchdown on every snap instead of stacking first downs. And just like football, that approach usually leads to mistakes.

Winning with stocks is not about highlights.

It is about execution.

## What Owning Stock Actually Means

When you buy a stock, you are not buying a ticker symbol, a logo, or a headline.

You are buying ownership in a real business.

That business sells products or services. It hires employees. It competes with other companies. It makes strategic decisions. It faces regulation, competition, and economic cycles. Over time, it either creates value or loses ground.

In football terms, owning stock is being part of the organization, not just cheering from the stands. You are tied to long-term performance, not one drive or one quarter.

This is where many people get it wrong.

They treat stocks like bets instead of ownership. They focus on short-term price movement instead of long-term business results. That mindset turns investing into gambling.

Stocks reward patience because businesses grow over time, not overnight.

## Why Stock Prices Move (And Why That Confuses People)

Stock prices move based on expectations.

Not just what a company did last quarter, but what investors believe it will do in the future. That creates volatility. News, earnings, rumors, and emotion all influence short-term pricing.

In football terms, this is weekly rankings.

They change constantly. A team moves up or down based on perception, not just results. The rankings do not determine who wins the championship. Execution does.

Price movement does not equal success or failure. It is just the market reacting to new information, often imperfectly.

## Growth vs Value Investing

Growth investing focuses on companies expected to grow faster than average.

These companies often reinvest profits instead of paying dividends. They expand aggressively. They get attention. They carry higher expectations and often higher volatility.

Value investing focuses on companies that are priced lower relative to fundamentals.

They may not be exciting. They may not dominate headlines. But they generate steady cash flow and tend to be more stable.

In football terms, growth is speed and explosiveness. Value is strength and fundamentals.

Championship teams need both.

A team built only on speed gets exposed when conditions change. A team built only on strength struggles to create separation. Balance matters.

Investors often make the mistake of picking a style instead of building a system.

## Dividends and Total Return

Dividends are cash payments some companies make to shareholders.

They provide income while you own the stock. They can be reinvested to buy more shares or used as cash flow. Dividends are real money, not just paper gains.

But dividends are only part of the picture.

Total return includes:

- Price appreciation
- Dividends received
- Reinvested dividends over time

Focusing on only one misses the full result.

In football terms, touchdowns matter. But so do field position, time of possession, and third-down conversions. The scoreboard reflects all of it.

Total return is the real measure of success.

## Why Athletes Are Drawn to Stock Hype

Athletes are wired to compete.

They are comfortable with pressure. They trust instincts. They have succeeded by taking risks. That mindset can be powerful, but it can also backfire in markets.

Stock hype speaks directly to athlete psychology:

- Big upside
- Confidence-based decisions
- Stories of fast success
- Fear of missing out

In football terms, hype is the trick play everyone talks about all week.

Sometimes it works. Most of the time it fails. And when it fails, it puts the team in a bad spot.

## Common Stock Market Myths Athletes Hear

Athletes hear a lot of bad advice about stocks.

"You have to trade constantly to win."

"You need inside information."

"If the price drops, you failed."

"Stocks are just gambling."

These myths come from misunderstanding how markets work.

Trading constantly increases mistakes and taxes. Inside information is illegal. Price drops are normal. And gambling is betting on outcomes. Investing is owning productive assets over time.

Football punishes freelancing.

Stocks do too.

## Why Boring Stocks Often Win

The most successful stock strategies are rarely exciting.

They focus on:

- Profitable businesses
- Competitive advantages
- Reasonable prices
- Long-term ownership

This approach feels slow. It feels boring. It feels uneventful.

In football terms, this is inside zone on third-and-two.

It does not make highlights. It moves the chains. It wins games.

Boring executed consistently beats exciting done occasionally.

## Coach's Perspective

A coach would say it directly.

Make the simple play.

Do your job.

Trust the system.

Stop trying to be the hero.

Coaches care about assignment discipline. Investors should too.

Stocks reward fundamentals, not flash.

## Game Situations and Decision Points

A stock drops in price.

Do you panic, or remember why you bought it?

You hear about a hot stock.

Do you chase it, or evaluate whether it fits your plan?

You feel bored.

Do you trade for excitement, or stay disciplined?

Same pressures. Same mistakes. Different field.

## Common Athlete Mistakes and Financial Parallels

Athletes chase highlights.

Financially, that means hype investing.

Athletes abandon the plan after one bad series.

Financially, that means panic selling.

Athletes overestimate instincts.

Financially, that means ignoring fundamentals.

Discipline fixes all three.

## Why Time Is the Real Advantage in Stocks

Time allows businesses to grow.

It allows earnings to compound. It allows dividends to stack. It allows mistakes to recover. It smooths volatility and rewards patience.

Athletes understand this better than most.

You did not get better overnight.

Your portfolio will not either.

The edge is not prediction.

The edge is staying invested.

## Winning the Long Game

Stocks are tools, not lottery tickets.

When used correctly, they build wealth slowly and steadily. When used emotionally, they create stress, regret, and frustration.

Execution beats excitement.

The teams that win championships are rarely the flashiest. They are the most disciplined.

## Athlete Takeaways

Owning stock means owning a real business.

Growth and value both play important roles.

Dividends plus price growth equal total return.

Hype is not a strategy.

Make the simple play, trust the system, and stay disciplined.

# Chapter 12: Bonds and Playing Defense in Your Portfolio

Every team loves offense, but no coach builds a game plan without defense.

You can score all you want, but if you cannot get stops, the game gets out of hand fast. Explosive offenses sell tickets. Defense wins championships. Defense controls momentum, shortens the game, protects leads, and keeps mistakes from becoming disasters.

Defense is not about excitement.

It is about control.

Bonds play that exact role in a portfolio.

They are not flashy. They do not get headlines. Nobody brags about them at a barbecue. But when markets get chaotic, bonds provide structure, stability, and discipline. They keep small mistakes from turning into season-ending losses.

Ignoring bonds is like running a no-defense game plan and hoping you never fall behind.

## How Bonds Work

A bond is a loan.

When you buy a bond, you are lending money to a government or a company. In exchange, the borrower agrees to pay you interest and return your original investment at a specific date called maturity.

That structure is intentional. Bonds are designed to be predictable.

In football terms, bonds are clock control. You are not trying to score fast. You are trying to manage the game, limit risk, and stay ahead of the chains.

Bonds exist to:

- Reduce volatility
- Provide income
- Preserve capital
- Add stability to a broader strategy

They are not designed to be exciting. They are designed to be reliable.

## Why Bonds Are Often Undervalued

Athletes and competitive people tend to undervalue bonds.

They look at returns. They compare numbers. They see stocks outperforming and assume bonds are dead weight. That mindset misses the point.

In football terms, this is focusing only on highlight plays. The deep ball looks great on film, but it does not matter if you cannot convert third down or protect a lead.

Bonds are not there to outperform stocks.

They are there to support them.

Most investing mistakes do not happen because someone chose the wrong asset. They happen because someone could not handle volatility and abandoned the plan at the wrong time. Bonds reduce the emotional pressure that causes those mistakes.

## Interest Rate Risk and Credit Risk

Two risks matter most with bonds.

### *Interest Rate Risk*

When interest rates rise, bond prices tend to fall. When interest rates fall, bond prices tend to rise.

This is not a flaw. It is part of how bonds work.

In football terms, this is field position. Sometimes conditions change. You adjust strategy accordingly. You do not panic because the wind shifted.

### *Credit Risk*

Credit risk is the risk that the borrower does not repay the loan.

Governments and strong companies usually carry lower credit risk. Weaker borrowers often offer higher interest to compensate for higher risk.

Higher yield usually means higher risk.

In football terms, this is situational awareness. You do not call the same play against every opponent. You assess the matchup.

Understanding risk allows bonds to play their role instead of surprising you.

## When Bonds Make Sense

Bonds matter most when stability matters.

They tend to play a larger role:

- When you are closer to using the money
- When income becomes more important than growth
- When volatility would force bad decisions
- When protecting progress matters more than maximizing upside

You do not eliminate offense. You balance it.

Younger athletes often dismiss bonds because they feel invincible and far from their goals. Older athletes often wish they had understood risk control earlier.

In football terms, this is veteran awareness. Late in the game, you protect the ball. You do not force throws just because you can.

Timing determines fit.

## Why Bonds Help You Stay Disciplined

Most people think investing failure comes from bad choices.

More often, it comes from emotional reactions.

Fear during downturns.

Overconfidence during rallies.

Impatience when progress feels slow.

Bonds reduce those emotional swings.

When part of your portfolio is stable, you are less likely to panic. You are more likely to stick to the plan. That discipline is what allows growth assets to do their job over time.

In football terms, bonds are a strong defense that lets the offense stay aggressive without pressing.

## Stability in a Diversified Portfolio

Diversification is not about maximizing returns. It is about managing risk.

Stocks provide growth.

Bonds provide stability.

Cash provides flexibility.

Each has a role.

In football terms, this is complementary football. Offense, defense, and special teams working together. Remove one unit and the system breaks down.

A portfolio with only stocks relies entirely on offense. When things go wrong, there is no support.

Balance creates resilience.

## Why Balanced Portfolios Feel Boring but Work

Balanced portfolios often feel dull.

Some assets are always lagging. Others are always leading. Nothing feels exciting. That boredom is not failure. It is function.

In football terms, clean games rarely feel chaotic. They feel controlled.

If your portfolio constantly feels exciting, something is probably off.

## Coach's Perspective

A coach would say it clearly.

Protect the lead.

Do not beat yourself.

Play smart.

Win situational football.

Defense is what allows you to close games.

Bonds help investors do the same.

## Game Situations and Decision Points

Markets get volatile.

Do you want protection or pure offense?

You are approaching a major financial goal.

Do you reduce risk or keep pressing?

You feel bored with stability.

Do you abandon defense or trust the plan?

These are not theory questions. They are in-game decisions.

## Common Athlete Mistakes and Financial Parallels

Athletes ignore defense.

Financially, that means ignoring bonds.

Athletes chase excitement.

Financially, that means excess risk.

Athletes misjudge the situation.

Financially, that means poor timing.

Championship teams respect defense.

## Winning the Long Game

Bonds do not win games by themselves.

They prevent you from losing them.

They limit damage.

They protect progress.

They support discipline.

Long-term success is not about scoring fast. It is about staying upright long enough for skill and patience to compound.

That is what defense does.

## Athlete Takeaways

- Bonds are loans, not bets
- Interest rate and credit risk matter
- Bonds provide stability when it counts
- Balance offense and defense
- Championships require control

# Chapter 13: Funds, ETFs, and Team-Based Investing

No coach builds a team with one player.

You need a full roster. Different positions. Different skill sets. Linemen who do the dirty work. Skill players who create opportunities. Depth players who keep the system intact when injuries happen.

Even the most talented athlete fails when asked to do everything alone.

Investing works the same way.

Funds and ETFs are team-based investing. Instead of relying on one company, one idea, or one perfect decision, you own a group of investments working together. Responsibility is spread. Risk is shared. Execution becomes more consistent.

That is how championships are won. Not with hero ball, but with systems that hold under pressure.

## Why Individual Stock Picking Breaks Down

Athletes are wired to trust themselves.

You have competed your entire life. You believe you can read situations, anticipate outcomes, and adjust. That mindset works on the field. It often fails in the market.

Picking individual stocks requires:

- Correct analysis
- Correct timing
- Emotional discipline
- Ongoing monitoring
- Willingness to admit mistakes quickly

Most people underestimate how hard that is.

In football terms, this is asking one player to play every position. Even great athletes break down under that load. One missed assignment creates exposure.

Funds and ETFs reduce the burden. You are no longer betting on one outcome. You are running a system.

## Mutual Funds vs ETFs

Mutual funds and ETFs both pool money from many investors and invest in a diversified collection of stocks or bonds.

The difference is how they operate.

Mutual funds typically:

- Trade once per day
- Are often actively managed
- May have higher minimums
- Can generate more taxable activity

ETFs typically:

- Trade throughout the day like stocks
- Are often index-based
- Tend to be more tax efficient
- Have lower minimum investment barriers

In football terms, mutual funds are structured practices. Reps are controlled.

Execution happens on a set schedule.

ETFs are game-speed reps. Faster. More flexible. More transparent.

Both can work. The key is understanding how they fit your system and behavior.

## Index vs Active Strategies

Index strategies aim to match the performance of a market or segment. Active strategies try to outperform through selection, timing, and decision-making.

Index investing emphasizes:

- Discipline
- Low cost
- Consistency
- Predictability

Active investing emphasizes:

- Manager judgment
- Strategy shifts
- Opportunity selection
- Higher potential variance

In football terms, index investing is running the base offense. It may not be flashy, but it works when executed consistently.

Active investing is calling audibles. Audibles can succeed, but only when players understand the situation and execute cleanly. Too many audibles create confusion.

Most athletes perform better when the system is clear and repeatable.

## Why Discipline Beats Brilliance

The market does not reward intelligence alone.

It rewards discipline.

Funds and ETFs remove many of the decisions that cause mistakes:

- When to buy
- When to sell
- What to rotate into
- How to react to headlines

You are not trying to outsmart the market. You are staying aligned with it.

In football terms, this is assignment football. Everyone does their job. Nobody freelances. The defense holds.

## Fees and Expense Ratios

Fees quietly decide outcomes.

Expense ratios are the cost of running a fund. They may look small on paper, but they compound year after year. That drag never takes a break.

In football terms, fees are penalties.

One holding call may not matter. A few false starts might be manageable. But constant penalties kill drives.

High fees do the same thing to portfolios. They reduce progress without you feeling the hit immediately.

Lower costs keep more of your effort working for you.

## Why Fees Matter More Than Performance Chasing

Many athletes chase performance without understanding cost.

They jump into funds with impressive recent returns but ignore fees. That often means paying more for yesterday's success.

In football terms, this is chasing last week's matchup. The film already changed.

Cost control is one of the few things investors can actually control. Use it.

## Diversification Without Complexity

Diversification spreads risk across many investments.

The goal is not to own everything. The goal is coverage.

You do not need dozens of funds. You need intentional exposure:

- Different sectors
- Different geographies
- Different asset types

In football terms, this is zone defense. Everyone covers their assignment. Nobody chases the same receiver. Gaps disappear.

Complexity creates mistakes. Simplicity creates execution.

## Why Team-Based Investing Reduces Emotional Errors

Most financial damage is emotional, not mathematical.

Fear during downturns. Overconfidence during rallies. Boredom leading to unnecessary trades.

Funds and ETFs reduce those emotional triggers.

You are less likely to:

- Panic sell
- Chase hype
- Overtrade
- Constantly second-guess decisions

In football terms, this is trusting the call and staying on assignment even when the crowd gets loud.

## Coach's Perspective

A coach would say it plainly.

Trust the system.

Do your job.

Do not overcomplicate it.

Win with fundamentals.

Funds exist to simplify execution under pressure.

## Game Situations and Decision Points

You want excitement.

Do you chase individual stocks or run a team strategy?

You hear about a high-fee fund.

Do you understand what it costs over time?

You feel behind.

Do you complicate the plan or stay disciplined?

Same pressures. Same decisions.

## Common Athlete Mistakes and Financial Parallels

Athletes try to do too much.

Financially, that leads to overtrading.

Athletes ignore fundamentals.

Financially, that leads to high fees.

Athletes chase stars.

Financially, that leads to poor diversification.

Championship teams avoid these traps.

## Winning the Long Game

Team-based investing works because it removes ego.

You do not need to be right about everything. You do not need perfect timing. You do not need inside information.

You need structure. Discipline. Time.

Funds and ETFs keep you in the game long enough for consistency to win.

## Athlete Takeaways

- Funds and ETFs are team-based investing
- Index strategies reward discipline
- Fees compound just like returns
- Diversification reduces mistakes
- Simple systems outperform complicated ones

# Chapter 14: Real Estate and Alternative Plays

Every team has specialty packages.

Goal-line defense.

Two-minute offense.

Trick plays drawn up for very specific moments.

They exist for a reason. They can change outcomes when used correctly. But no coach installs specialty packages before the team understands the basics. If players do not know assignments, timing, and fundamentals, specialty plays turn into disasters.

Real estate and alternative investments work the same way.

They can add value. They can create opportunity. They can strengthen a long-term plan. But when they are used too early or without understanding, they create risk instead of results.

These are not foundation pieces. They are situational tools.

## Why Athletes Are Drawn to Specialty Investments

Athletes are wired to seek advantage.

You have spent your life looking for edges. Extra reps. Better training. Faster recovery. That mindset is powerful. It can also backfire financially.

Real estate and alternatives often sound like edges:

- "This is how real money is made."

- "Stocks are slow."
- "This is what wealthy people do."
- "You need multiple income streams."

Those statements are not always wrong. They are often mistimed.

In football terms, this is calling a trick play because you are bored with the base offense. It works sometimes. When it fails, it costs field position and momentum.

## Renting vs Owning

Renting provides flexibility.

Owning provides stability and long-term potential.

Neither is a trophy. Neither is a failure.

Renting is like being on a one-year deal. You can relocate quickly. You are not responsible for repairs. You preserve flexibility if income changes or opportunities arise.

Owning is like signing a long-term contract. You build equity. You control the environment. You commit to location, maintenance, and ongoing costs.

There is no universal right answer.

The decision depends on:

- Income stability
- Career flexibility
- Location
- Time horizon
- Willingness to manage responsibility

Buying before you are ready is like committing to a scheme that does not fit your personnel. The playbook might look good, but execution suffers.

## The Hidden Costs of Ownership

Many athletes focus on the upside of owning and underestimate the responsibility.

Ownership includes:

- Maintenance
- Repairs
- Property taxes
- Insurance
- Unexpected expenses
- Reduced flexibility

In football terms, this is playing through an injury without depth. You can survive, but mistakes hurt more.

Ownership can be a strong move when it fits. It becomes a burden when it does not.

## REITs and Indirect Ownership

REITs allow you to invest in real estate without owning property directly.

You get exposure to real estate income and appreciation without managing tenants, repairs, or leverage.

In football terms, this is being part of the organization without running operations. You benefit from the system without carrying the full load.

REITs can:

- Provide income
- Add diversification
- Reduce operational stress

They also carry market risk. Prices move. Income can fluctuate. They are not guaranteed.

REITs often make more sense early than direct property ownership because they preserve liquidity and simplicity.

## Alternatives Like Commodities and Private Investments

Alternatives include:

- Commodities
- Private equity
- Private credit
- Hedge strategies
- Other non-traditional assets

They can provide diversification and opportunity. They also come with trade-offs.

Alternatives are often:

- Complex
- Illiquid
- Expensive
- Difficult to value
- Hard to exit

In football terms, these are trick plays. When timed well and executed cleanly, they can change momentum. When forced, they create turnovers.

Most athletes do not need alternatives early. Fundamentals matter more than complexity.

## Why Alternatives Are Often Overused

Alternatives appeal to ego.

They feel sophisticated. They sound exclusive. They promise access and advantage. That attraction leads people to use them before they are ready.

In football terms, this is installing trick plays before players understand base assignments. The result is confusion under pressure.

Alternatives should complement a strong foundation, not replace it.

## Liquidity and Risk Considerations

Liquidity is how quickly you can access your money.

Stocks and bonds are generally liquid. Real estate and alternatives often are not.

When money is illiquid:

- Selling may take time
- Prices may be unfavorable
- Options become limited

In football terms, this is field position. You cannot always reverse field. You cannot always escape pressure.

Before committing to illiquid investments, ask:

- When might I need this money?
- What happens if income changes?
- What if life forces an adjustment?

Ignoring liquidity is one of the fastest ways athletes get trapped financially.

## Why Liquidity Equals Flexibility

Flexibility creates options.

Options reduce stress.

Stress leads to mistakes.

Illiquid investments can be powerful when planned correctly. They can also create pressure when life changes unexpectedly.

Strong teams value flexibility. Strong financial plans do too.

## Coach's Perspective

A coach would be clear.

Master the basics first.

Know the situation.

Do not force specialty plays.

Protect flexibility.

Specialty investments belong in the right moment, not because they sound impressive.

## Game Situations and Decision Points

You want to buy property.

Do you understand the full commitment?

You hear about a private deal.

Do you understand liquidity and risk?

You feel bored with steady progress.

Do you add complexity or stay disciplined?

Timing matters.

## Common Athlete Mistakes and Financial Parallels

Athletes rush into new roles.

Financially, that means premature complexity.

Athletes underestimate recovery time.

Financially, that means liquidity problems.

Athletes chase excitement.

Financially, that means unnecessary risk.

Championship teams avoid forcing plays.

## Winning the Long Game

Real estate and alternatives are not shortcuts.

They are tools.

When used intentionally, they can strengthen a plan. When used emotionally, they create imbalance.

The goal is not to collect assets. The goal is to build a system that holds up when pressure hits.

Master the basics first. Then layer complexity when it fits.

## Athlete Takeaways

- Renting and owning serve different purposes
- REITs offer indirect exposure without operations
- Alternatives add complexity and risk
- Liquidity matters more than people think
- Master fundamentals before specialty plays

# Part IV: Managing the Season (Portfolio Management)

**Winning is about adjustments, not perfection.**

No season goes exactly as planned.

Injuries happen. Roles change. Opponents adjust. What worked in Week 1 rarely works the same way in Week 10. The teams that survive are not the ones chasing perfection. They are the ones making smart adjustments without abandoning their identity.

Money works the same way.

Your financial plan is not something you set once and forget. It is something you manage. Review. Adjust. Then recommit to. Not every dip is a problem. Not every change requires action. Knowing the difference is the skill.

Most investing mistakes do not come from bad plans. They come from bad reactions.

Overreacting to noise.

Panicking during volatility.

Tinkering out of boredom.

Ignoring real life changes.

Managing the season means staying engaged without overcoaching.

In this section, you will learn how to review your portfolio the right way. How to rebalance without emotion. How to adjust when life changes without blowing up the plan. And how to stay disciplined when markets test your patience.

This is situational football.

You do not abandon the playbook because of one bad drive. You do not force changes because of outside noise. You trust the preparation, make calculated adjustments, and keep playing.

Winning over a full season requires consistency, awareness, and restraint.

That is what this section teaches.

Stay focused.

Stay disciplined.

Make adjustments when they matter.

That is how you finish strong.

# Chapter 15: Asset Allocation: Building the Right Lineup

Every team has specialty packages.

Goal-line defense.

Two-minute offense.

Trick plays drawn up for very specific moments.

They exist for a reason. Used correctly, they can change outcomes. They can steal momentum. They can flip a game when timing and execution are right.

But no coach installs specialty packages before the team understands the basics.

If players do not know assignments, timing, and fundamentals, specialty plays turn into disasters. Missed blocks. Blown coverages. Turnovers at the worst possible moment.

Real estate and alternative investments work the same way.

They can add value. They can create opportunity. They can strengthen a long-term financial plan. But when they are used too early, or without understanding, they create risk instead of results.

These are not foundation pieces.

They are situational tools.

## Why Athletes Are Drawn to Specialty Investments

Athletes are wired to seek advantage.

You have spent your entire life looking for edges. Extra reps. Better training methods. Faster recovery. Film study. Nutrition. Sleep. Marginal gains add up in sports, and that mindset has helped you compete.

That same mindset can be powerful financially. It can also backfire.

Real estate and alternative investments often get marketed as "the edge":

- "This is how real money is made."
- "Stocks are slow."
- "This is what wealthy people do."
- "You need multiple income streams."

Those statements are not always wrong. But they are often mistimed.

In football terms, this is calling a trick play because you are bored with the base offense. It works sometimes. When it fails, it costs field position, momentum, and confidence.

Specialty investments feel proactive. They feel advanced. They feel like you are doing something smart.

But doing something advanced too early is not smart. It is risky.

## Renting vs Owning

Renting provides flexibility.

Owning provides stability and long-term potential.

Neither is a trophy.

Neither is a failure.

Renting is like being on a one-year deal. You can relocate quickly. You are not responsible for major repairs. You preserve flexibility if income changes or opportunities arise.

Owning is like signing a long-term contract. You build equity. You control your environment. You commit to location, maintenance, and ongoing costs whether income is stable or not.

There is no universal right answer.

The decision depends on:

- Income stability
- Career flexibility
- Location
- Time horizon
- Willingness to manage responsibility

Buying before you are ready is like committing to a scheme that does not fit your personnel. The playbook might look good on paper, but execution suffers when reality hits.

## The Hidden Costs of Ownership

Many athletes focus on the upside of owning and underestimate the responsibility.

Ownership includes:

- Maintenance
- Repairs
- Property taxes
- Insurance
- Unexpected expenses
- Reduced flexibility

These costs do not show up evenly. They show up when timing is bad.

In football terms, this is playing through an injury without depth behind you. You can survive, but mistakes hurt more and recovery takes longer.

Ownership can be a strong move when it fits your situation. It becomes a burden when it does not.

The question is not "Can I buy?"

The question is "Does this fit my current season of life?"

## REITs and Indirect Ownership

REITs allow you to invest in real estate without owning property directly.

You get exposure to real estate income and appreciation without dealing with tenants, maintenance calls, or leverage.

In football terms, this is being part of the organization without running operations. You benefit from the system without carrying the full load.

REITs can:

- Provide income
- Add diversification
- Reduce operational stress

They also carry market risk. Prices move. Income can fluctuate. They are not guaranteed.

REITs often make more sense earlier than direct property ownership because they preserve liquidity and simplicity. You stay invested without locking yourself into long-term commitments you cannot easily adjust.

## Alternatives Like Commodities and Private Investments

Alternatives include:

- Commodities
- Private equity
- Private credit
- Hedge strategies
- Other non-traditional assets

They can provide diversification and opportunity. They also come with serious trade-offs.

Alternatives are often:

- Complex
- Illiquid
- Expensive
- Difficult to value
- Hard to exit

In football terms, these are trick plays. When timed well and executed cleanly, they can change momentum. When forced, they create turnovers.

Most athletes do not need alternatives early. Fundamentals matter more than complexity.

## Why Alternatives Are Often Overused

Alternatives appeal to ego.

They feel sophisticated. They sound exclusive. They promise access and advantage. That attraction pushes people to use them before they are ready.

In football terms, this is installing trick plays before players understand base assignments. When pressure hits, confusion follows.

Alternatives should complement a strong foundation, not replace it.

If the base offense is not sound, trick plays do not save you.

## Liquidity and Risk Considerations

Liquidity is how quickly you can access your money.

Stocks and bonds are generally liquid. Real estate and alternatives often are not.

When money is illiquid:

- Selling may take time
- Prices may be unfavorable
- Options become limited

In football terms, this is field position. You cannot always reverse field. You cannot always escape pressure.

Before committing to illiquid investments, ask:

- When might I need this money?
- What happens if income changes?
- What if life forces an adjustment?

Ignoring liquidity is one of the fastest ways athletes get trapped financially.

## Why Liquidity Equals Flexibility

Flexibility creates options.

Options reduce stress.

Stress leads to mistakes.

Illiquid investments can be powerful when planned correctly. They can also create pressure when life changes unexpectedly.

Strong teams value flexibility.

Strong financial plans do too.

## Coach's Perspective

A coach would be clear.

Master the basics first.

Know the situation.

Do not force specialty plays.

Protect flexibility.

Specialty investments belong in the right moment, not because they sound impressive.

## Game Situations and Decision Points

You want to buy property.

Do you understand the full commitment?

You hear about a private deal.

Do you understand liquidity and risk?

You feel bored with steady progress.

Do you add complexity or stay disciplined?

Timing matters.

## Common Athlete Mistakes and Financial Parallels

Athletes rush into new roles.

Financially, that means premature complexity.

Athletes underestimate recovery time.

Financially, that means liquidity problems.

Athletes chase excitement.

Financially, that means unnecessary risk.

Championship teams avoid forcing plays.

## Winning the Long Game

Real estate and alternative investments are not shortcuts.

They are tools.

When used intentionally, they can strengthen a plan. When used emotionally, they create imbalance.

The goal is not to collect assets.

The goal is to build a system that holds up when pressure hits.

Master the basics first.

Then layer complexity when it fits.

## Athlete Takeaways

- Renting and owning serve different purposes
- REITs offer indirect exposure without operations
- Alternatives add complexity and risk
- Liquidity matters more than people think
- Master fundamentals before specialty plays

# Chapter 16: Buying, Holding, and Staying Disciplined

Every player has felt this moment.

The crowd is loud. Momentum is swinging. Something just went wrong. A turnover. A blown assignment. A missed opportunity. Instinct screams do something right now. Change the call. Force the issue. Make a play to get it back.

Great coaches do the opposite.

They slow it down. They trust preparation. They lean on fundamentals. They stick with what works instead of reacting to noise. They know that panic creates bigger mistakes than the original problem ever did.

Buying and holding investments requires that same discipline.

Most investing mistakes are not about what people buy. They are about how people behave after they buy it. The plan is usually fine. The execution breaks down when emotions take over.

## Why Behavior Matters More Than Strategy

On paper, investing looks simple.

Choose a reasonable plan. Fund it consistently. Give it time. Let compounding work. Most people understand this intellectually. Very few follow it behaviorally.

Why?

Because markets create pressure without whistles.

Prices move constantly. Headlines are dramatic. Commentary is emotional. There is no coach calling timeout when panic sets in. You are expected to manage uncertainty quietly, without feedback, and without immediate validation.

That environment exposes weaknesses in discipline, not intelligence.

Buy-and-hold investing is not about being passive. It is about being patient when action feels urgent.

## Opening and Funding Accounts: Getting Lined Up Correctly

Before you can execute a game plan, you have to line up correctly.

Investment accounts are the infrastructure. Brokerage accounts. Retirement accounts. Employer plans. Automatic contributions. Beneficiary designations. Tax treatment. Access.

If this foundation is sloppy, execution becomes harder than it needs to be.

In football terms, this is pre-snap alignment.

You can have the best play in the book, but if you are lined up wrong, it fails. Missed assignments cause penalties. Confusion leads to blown plays. None of that has anything to do with effort.

The same is true with investing.

Accounts should be:

- Easy to fund
- Easy to monitor
- Easy to understand
- Easy to stay consistent with

Complexity creates friction. Friction creates delay. Delay creates inconsistency. Inconsistency kills results.

The goal is not sophistication. The goal is reliability.

Automatic contributions matter more than clever allocation tweaks. Simplicity matters more than optimization. Systems that work quietly outperform plans that look impressive but require constant attention.

## Why Setup Mistakes Lead to Long-Term Problems

Many investing struggles start before the first dollar is invested.

Accounts are opened but not funded. Contributions are irregular. Beneficiaries are forgotten. Logins are confusing. Statements are ignored. These are not strategy problems. They are setup problems.

In football terms, this is poor preparation during the week.

You do not see the damage immediately. The game still gets played. But when pressure hits, the lack of preparation shows up fast.

A clean setup reduces the number of decisions you have to make later. Fewer decisions mean fewer emotional mistakes.

## Market Orders vs Limit Orders: Knowing the Tools

A market order buys or sells immediately at the current available price.

A limit order sets a specific price and waits until that price is available.

Neither is right or wrong. They serve different purposes.

In football terms, a market order is snapping the ball and running the play as called.

A limit order is checking the defense, adjusting the play call, and waiting for the right matchup.

What matters is knowing which tool you are using and why.

Confusion creates frustration. Frustration leads to second-guessing. Second-guessing leads to bad decisions.

Most long-term investors do not need to obsess over order types. The real risk is not execution price on a single trade. The real risk is behavior over decades.

Understanding basics builds confidence. Confidence reduces overreaction.

## Buy-and-Hold Is Discipline, Not Inactivity

Buy-and-hold investing is often misunderstood.

It is not laziness. It is not ignoring reality. It is not refusing to think. It is choosing to let a plan work instead of constantly interfering with it.

Buy-and-hold means:

- You invest with a long-term plan
- You expect volatility
- You accept that progress is uneven
- You resist the urge to react to every movement
- You focus on outcomes measured in years, not weeks

In football terms, this is trusting the game plan for four quarters.

You do not abandon the run because of one bad series. You do not change the offense every time the defense adjusts. You execute, adjust within the plan, and stay patient.

Most wealth is built by staying invested, not by trading frequently.

Frequent trading feels productive. It feels like effort. But activity is not the same as progress.

## Why Doing Nothing Is Often the Hardest Play

Doing nothing feels wrong to athletes.

You are trained to respond. To adjust. To take action. Standing still under pressure feels like failure.

Markets exploit that instinct.

Volatility creates the illusion that something must be done. Red numbers trigger fear. Green numbers trigger excitement. Commentary amplifies urgency. Doing nothing feels irresponsible.

In reality, unnecessary action is often the most expensive mistake.

In football terms, this is pressing after a turnover.

You try to make a big play to fix a small problem. That leads to missed assignments, blown coverage, and bigger losses.

Buy-and-hold forces humility.

It removes ego. It removes the illusion of control. It asks you to accept that you cannot outsmart the system consistently. That is uncomfortable, but it is effective.

## Avoiding Emotional Play-Calling

Emotions cost money.

Fear during downturns leads to selling low. Greed during rallies leads to chasing highs. Boredom leads to unnecessary trades. Anxiety leads to abandoning good plans. Confidence leads to overconfidence.

Football teaches emotional control.

Next play. Eyes up. Stay composed. Do your job. Emotion is acknowledged, then set aside.

Money demands the same mindset.

Systems beat emotions. Automation beats panic. Discipline beats excitement.

If your plan requires you to feel calm at all times, it is a bad plan. The plan should work even when you do not feel calm.

## Why Automation Is a Competitive Advantage

Automation removes decision points.

Automatic contributions. Automatic rebalancing. Automatic investing. These systems work regardless of mood, headlines, or stress levels.

In football terms, this is tempo.

When the offense controls tempo, the defense has less opportunity to disrupt execution. Automation controls tempo in your financial life.

You are less likely to panic-sell if you are not manually moving money. You are less likely to chase hype if contributions happen automatically. You are less likely to overtrade if you do not need to log in constantly.

Automation does not eliminate risk. It eliminates unnecessary interference.

## Coach's Perspective on Discipline Under Pressure

A coach would say it clearly.

Trust the preparation.

Execute the plan.

Do not flinch.

Make the simple play.

Coaches know that games are rarely lost on one play. They are lost when teams abandon fundamentals under pressure.

Investing works the same way.

Emotional play-calling loses games. Disciplined execution wins them quietly.

## Game Situations and Decision Points

This is where buy-and-hold is tested.

Markets drop. Do you abandon the plan or stay invested?

You feel bored. Do you trade for excitement or stay disciplined?

You hear outside noise. Do you react to opinions or review your own plan?

You feel behind. Do you force action or stick with consistency?

These moments feel urgent. They are not.

Your response matters more than the market's movement.

## Common Athlete Mistakes and Financial Parallels

Athletes press when things go wrong.

Financially, that leads to panic selling.

Athletes chase momentum.

Financially, that leads to buying high.

Athletes overthink assignments.

Financially, that leads to overtrading.

Athletes abandon fundamentals under pressure.

Financially, that leads to abandoning long-term plans.

The pattern is the same.

## Why Buy-and-Hold Works Over Time

Buy-and-hold works because it removes the biggest threat to returns.

You.

Markets will do what markets do. Prices will move. Volatility will happen. Cycles will repeat. None of that is new.

What changes outcomes is whether you stay in the game.

Buy-and-hold keeps you invested long enough for compounding to matter. It reduces transaction costs. It minimizes taxes. It protects you from emotional mistakes. It forces patience.

You do not win by making every play.

You win by avoiding the mistakes that lose games.

## Reframing Inaction as Execution

Former athletes struggle because buy-and-hold feels like inaction.

Reframe it.

Buy-and-hold is executing the plan.

Staying invested is doing your job.

Ignoring noise is discipline.

Consistency is effort.

Execution does not always look like movement. Sometimes it looks like restraint.

That is a harder skill than action.

## Winning the Long Game

Buying and holding works because it rewards the traits athletes already have, once they are redirected correctly.

Preparation.

Patience.

Discipline.

Trust in the plan.

The difference is that the feedback loop is slower and quieter. There are no crowds. No scoreboards. No instant validation.

Just outcomes over time.

That is why so many people fail at it. Not because it is complex, but because it is boring and emotionally uncomfortable.

## Athlete Takeaways

Get aligned before you snap the ball.

Simple systems beat complex ones.

Know the difference between market and limit orders.

Buy-and-hold is disciplined, not passive.

Emotions are expensive. Systems are not.

Doing nothing is often the hardest and best play.

Trust the plan and execute through noise.

Great players do not win by forcing plays.

They win by staying disciplined when everyone else panics.

That same discipline is what makes buy-and-hold investing work.

# Chapter 17: Rebalancing and Halftime Adjustments

Halftime is not about panic.

You do not rip up the playbook because one drive went poorly. You also do not pretend everything is fine when it clearly is not. Halftime is where good teams separate themselves from reactive ones. You slow the game down. You watch the film. You identify what actually matters. Then you make a few intentional adjustments and leave the rest alone.

Rebalancing works the same way.

It is not about reacting to every movement in the market. It is about maintaining alignment with the game plan you built before emotions entered the picture. When done correctly, rebalancing feels calm, boring, and controlled. When done incorrectly, it feels frantic and destructive.

This chapter is about learning the difference.

## Why Rebalancing Exists at All

Markets move unevenly.

Some assets grow faster than others. Some lag. Some surge unexpectedly. Over time, those movements pull your portfolio away from its original design. Risk increases quietly. Exposure shifts without you noticing.

Rebalancing is the process of restoring balance.

It brings your portfolio back to its intended mix so risk, growth potential, and stability stay aligned with your goals. It is not about predicting markets.

It is about managing drift.

In sports terms, this is identity management.

Good teams know who they are. They know what they are built to do. When circumstances change, they make adjustments that reinforce identity instead of abandoning it.

Rebalancing protects identity.

## Why More Monitoring Usually Makes Things Worse

One of the biggest mistakes investors make is checking too often.

Daily monitoring feels responsible. It feels like paying attention. In reality, it usually creates stress, not clarity. Small movements feel big. Noise feels meaningful. Emotion creeps in.

In football terms, this is trying to coach during every play.

You cannot evaluate performance mid-snap. You cannot see patterns while the game is still unfolding. You end up reacting to moments instead of managing strategy.

Film review happens after the fact for a reason.

Most long-term investors only need to review portfolios quarterly or annually unless something significant changes. That cadence creates perspective. It allows trends to emerge. It separates signal from noise.

More checking does not improve outcomes.

It increases interference.

## Rebalancing Is Not Trading

This distinction matters.

Trading is reactive. It responds to price movement, headlines, and emotion. Rebalancing is intentional. It responds to allocation drift relative to a plan.

Rebalancing asks one simple question:

Does my portfolio still match my original strategy?

If the answer is no, adjustments are made to restore balance. Not to chase performance. Not to avoid fear. Not to predict what comes next.

In football terms, this is rotating personnel, not changing the offense.

You are not abandoning the system. You are keeping it functional.

## How Rebalancing Actually Works

Over time, assets grow at different rates.

If stocks perform well, they can grow into a larger percentage of your portfolio than intended. That increases risk. If bonds outperform, your portfolio may become more conservative than planned, slowing long-term growth.

Rebalancing corrects this by selling portions of what has grown beyond its target and adding to what has lagged.

This feels counterintuitive emotionally.

You are trimming winners and adding to underperformers. Emotionally, people want to do the opposite. That emotional resistance is exactly why rebalancing works.

In sports terms, this is workload management.

You rest players who have carried heavy loads. You develop others to maintain balance. You do not run one player into the ground just because they had a great quarter.

Rebalancing is disciplined selling and buying, not emotional trading.

## Timing Rebalancing Without Overdoing It

There are two common approaches to rebalancing.

Time-based rebalancing reviews the portfolio on a set schedule, such as annually. Allocation-based rebalancing triggers adjustments when holdings drift beyond predetermined ranges.

Both approaches work. What matters is consistency.

Rebalancing too frequently increases costs, taxes, and emotional involvement. Rebalancing too infrequently allows risk to drift unchecked.

In football terms, this is halftime and bye-week adjustments.

You do not adjust every drive. You do not wait an entire season to correct obvious problems. You choose moments that allow perspective.

The goal is not perfect balance at all times.

The goal is reasonable alignment over time.

## Life Changes Matter More Than Market Moves

The most important adjustments are rarely driven by markets.

They are driven by life.

New job.

Income changes.

Marriage.

Children.

Home purchases.

Career shifts.

Health changes.

These events alter your risk capacity, time horizon, and priorities. Ignoring them while obsessing over market movement is backwards.

In football terms, this is running last year's playbook with a new roster.

Personnel changes require strategy adjustments. Ignoring reality creates breakdowns that no amount of discipline can fix.

Rebalancing after life changes is not optional.

It is necessary.

## Why Ignoring Life Changes Is So Costly

Many investors stick with outdated strategies because changing feels uncomfortable.

They assume the plan that worked before will keep working. They delay updates because everything feels fine in the moment.

Then stress appears later.

Risk feels too high when responsibilities increase. Growth feels too slow when goals accelerate. Misalignment creates anxiety that shows up as second-guessing and emotional decisions.

This is not a market problem.

It is a management problem.

## Avoiding Over-Coaching and Over-Tinkering

Over-coaching ruins teams.

Too many adjustments. Too many voices. Too much tinkering. Players lose confidence. Identity disappears. Execution breaks down.

In investing, over-coaching looks like:

Constant trading.

Reacting to headlines.

Second-guessing allocation.

Changing strategies after short-term underperformance.

Chasing what just worked.

These behaviors feel proactive. They are not.

They are interference.

Good coaches make fewer adjustments and make them well. They know the difference between noise and signal.

Investing requires the same restraint.

## Why Tinkering Feels So Tempting

Tinkering creates the illusion of control.

Doing something feels better than sitting still. Adjusting feels like engagement. But engagement without direction causes damage.

In sports, this shows up when coaches outthink themselves.

In investing, it shows up when investors confuse activity with improvement.

Most of the time, the best adjustment is patience.

## Rebalancing as Forced Discipline

Rebalancing does something important psychologically.

It forces you to act against instinct.

You sell what feels good.

You buy what feels uncomfortable.

You restore balance instead of chasing excitement.

This discipline is what keeps portfolios aligned through cycles.

In football terms, this is sticking with fundamentals under pressure.

You do not abandon your identity because the crowd is loud. You do not force plays because momentum feels off.

You execute the plan.

## Coach's Perspective on Halftime Adjustments

A coach would be clear.

Trust the preparation.

Make smart adjustments.

Do not panic.

Stick to the identity.

Halftime is about clarity, not chaos.

Rebalancing should feel the same way. Calm. Intentional. Grounded in a long-term plan.

## Game Situations and Decision Points

Rebalancing is tested in specific moments.

Markets move sharply. Do you rebalance or overreact?

Your life changes. Do you update the plan or ignore it?

You feel the urge to tinker. Do you step back or interfere?

Performance diverges from expectations. Do you review or panic?

These are management moments, not emotional ones.

Your response determines whether discipline holds or breaks.

## Common Athlete Mistakes and Financial Parallels

Athletes panic at halftime.

Financially, that leads to reactive trading.

Athletes overcorrect after one mistake.

Financially, that leads to unnecessary risk changes.

Athletes ignore roster changes.

Financially, that leads to outdated strategies.

The parallel is consistent.

Poor adjustments do more damage than standing still.

## Why Rebalancing Supports Buy-and-Hold

Buy-and-hold does not mean ignore forever.

It means adjust with intention instead of emotion.

Rebalancing is how buy-and-hold stays relevant over time. It keeps the portfolio aligned without abandoning the long-term approach. It allows adaptation without panic.

In sports terms, this is halftime coaching that reinforces identity instead of rewriting it.

## The Psychological Benefit of a Rebalancing Plan

Having a defined rebalancing process reduces anxiety.

You know when to act.

You know when not to act.

You stop guessing.

You stop reacting to noise.

That clarity is powerful.

Most investing stress comes from uncertainty about what to do. A rebalancing framework removes that uncertainty.

You are no longer improvising.

You are managing.

## Winning the Long Game

Rebalancing keeps you aligned.

It prevents drift.

It enforces discipline.

It manages risk.

It supports consistency.

Smart adjustments win seasons. Not constant changes. Not panic reactions.

The teams that succeed long-term are the ones that stay true to their identity while making necessary, thoughtful corrections along the way.

Portfolios work the same way.

## Athlete Takeaways

Halftime is for clarity, not panic.

Review investments with purpose, not obsession.

Rebalancing restores balance and manages risk.

Life changes matter more than market noise.

Over-coaching creates mistakes.

Discipline is sticking to the plan while making smart adjustments.

You do not win by reacting to every play.

You win by managing the game.

Rebalancing is how you do that in investing.

# Chapter 18: The Mental Game of Money

Every athlete knows this feeling.

You make one mistake. The crowd reacts. Momentum shifts. Your heart rate spikes. The next play is coming fast, and your mind wants to replay what just happened instead of focusing on what comes next. If you stay stuck on the mistake, another one is almost guaranteed.

Great players reset.

They breathe. They refocus. They trust their preparation. They line up and play the next snap.

Money creates the same pressure.

Markets move quickly. Headlines are dramatic. Opinions are loud and conflicting. Friends, coworkers, and media all have takes. Emotions spike. And just like football, the mental game often determines the outcome more than talent, intelligence, or access to information.

This chapter is about that mental game. Because most financial mistakes are not caused by lack of knowledge. They are caused by loss of emotional control.

## Why the Mental Side of Money Is So Hard

Athletes are trained to manage emotion under pressure.

You learn to control adrenaline. You learn to respond instead of react. You learn that one play does not define the game. Those skills are transferable, but the environment around money is very different.

In sports, pressure is structured.

There is a play clock. There is a whistle. There is a coach. There is a clear objective on the next snap. In markets, pressure is unstructured. There is no whistle. There is no timeout. Information never stops. Opinions never stop. And no one tells you when to act or when to stand still.

That constant pressure exposes emotional weaknesses quickly.

## Fear, Greed, and Overconfidence

Three emotions dominate financial behavior.

Fear makes you freeze.

Greed makes you chase.

Overconfidence makes you ignore risk.

All three show up repeatedly in markets.

Fear causes people to sell when prices are already down. Loss feels unbearable, so people lock it in. The decision feels like relief in the moment, but it creates long-term damage.

Greed shows up when things are going well. People chase what is hot. They buy things they do not understand because they do not want to miss out. Excitement overrides discipline.

Overconfidence shows up after success. A few good decisions turn into belief that the rules no longer apply. Risk is underestimated. Concentration increases. Mistakes follow.

In football terms, these are mental penalties.

False starts. Late hits. Unforced errors. None of them are about ability. They are about emotional control.

The best athletes are not emotionless.

They are disciplined.

They feel everything. They just do not let feelings dictate behavior.

## Why Fear Is So Powerful With Money

Fear is tied to survival.

Money represents security. Safety. Control. When markets drop, the brain does not see percentages. It sees threat. That triggers fight, flight, or freeze responses.

Selling during fear feels like taking control. In reality, it is often the worst possible time to act.

In football terms, this is panicking after a turnover.

You want to make up for it immediately. You force a throw. You press. You compound the mistake.

Fear narrows perspective. It makes short-term pain feel more important than long-term goals. That is why fear-based decisions are so costly.

## Why Greed Feels Rational in the Moment

Greed rarely feels like greed.

It feels like opportunity. It feels like confidence. It feels like being smart enough to see something others are missing.

That is what makes it dangerous.

When everyone around you is talking about gains, staying disciplined feels foolish. Sitting still feels like falling behind. Greed convinces you that this time is different.

In football terms, this is chasing momentum instead of executing the game plan.

You abandon what works because the crowd is loud and the moment feels big. You try to hit the home run instead of moving the chains.

Greed is not loud panic.

It is quiet justification.

## Overconfidence and the Illusion of Control

Overconfidence is often the final stage.

After a period of success, people start to believe outcomes are the result of skill alone. Luck is dismissed. Risk is minimized. Concentration increases. Safeguards get removed.

This is where damage can be severe.

In football terms, this is abandoning fundamentals because things have been going well. You stop wrapping up tackles. You freelance. You assume the opponent cannot hurt you.

Markets punish overconfidence ruthlessly.

No one is immune to cycles. No one is above risk. Overconfidence creates blind spots that only show up after it is too late.

## Herd Mentality and the Power of Noise

Crowds influence behavior.

Humans are wired to seek safety in numbers. When everyone is panicking, staying calm feels unsafe. When everyone is excited, staying disciplined feels lonely.

Markets amplify this effect.

Social media. News cycles. Group chats. Online forums. Constant commentary makes it feel like everyone is doing something. Doing nothing feels irresponsible.

In football terms, this is getting caught up in the noise instead of listening to the coach.

The crowd reacts to every play. Coaches focus on the game plan. Players who listen to the crowd lose focus. Teams that tune out noise execute better.

Herd behavior replaces thinking with reacting.

That is expensive.

## Why Intelligence Does Not Protect You

One of the most surprising truths about money is that intelligence does not prevent emotional mistakes.

Highly educated people panic. Experienced professionals chase trends. Smart athletes make poor financial decisions.

Why?

Because emotion bypasses logic under pressure.

Knowledge helps only if systems exist to support it. Without structure, even the smartest people fall into predictable emotional traps.

This is why discipline must be designed, not hoped for.

## Building Systems for Discipline

Discipline does not come from willpower.

Willpower fades. Stress drains it. Emotion overrides it. Systems create consistency when feelings are unreliable.

Strong financial systems include:

Automatic contributions that happen regardless of mood.

Clear rules for when and how rebalancing occurs.

Defined goals with timelines attached.

Boundaries that limit impulsive decisions.

In football terms, this is routine.

Warmups. Film study. Practice habits. These systems exist so performance does not depend on how you feel that day.

You do not rely on motivation to train.

You rely on structure.

Money deserves the same respect.

## Why Systems Beat Emotions Every Time

Systems remove decision points.

When fewer decisions are required, fewer emotional mistakes are possible. Automation eliminates hesitation. Rules eliminate debate. Structure eliminates panic.

In football terms, this is tempo.

When tempo is controlled, execution improves. When chaos takes over, mistakes multiply.

A good system works quietly in the background. It does not care about headlines. It does not get excited. It does not get scared.

That is the point.

## Staying Focused During Market Chaos

Market chaos is normal.

Corrections happen. Bear markets happen. Volatility spikes. Headlines turn negative. These are features of markets, not flaws.

The question is not whether chaos will happen.

It is how you respond when it does.

In football terms, this is adversity.

Every game includes it. Good teams expect it. They prepare for it. They do not let it define them.

Chaos exposes weak systems.

Strong systems hold.

If your plan requires calm emotions to work, it is not a good plan. A good plan works even when emotions are loud.

## The Reset Skill

One of the most valuable skills athletes learn is the reset.

Bad play. Reset.

Missed assignment. Reset.

Dropped pass. Reset.

You do not carry the mistake into the next snap.

Money requires the same skill.

You will make mistakes. Everyone does. The damage comes from what happens next. Do you spiral? Do you press? Do you abandon discipline? Or do you reset?

Resetting means returning to the plan.

Not punishing yourself. Not overcorrecting. Not quitting.

Just next play.

## Coach's Perspective on Mental Toughness

A coach would be blunt.

Control what you can control.

Next play.

Stay locked in.

Do not flinch.

Mental toughness wins close games.

Not raw talent. Not flashy plays. Not emotion.

Discipline under pressure is the difference.

## Game Situations and Decision Points

This mental game shows up in specific moments.

Markets drop suddenly. Do you panic or stick to the plan?

You hear everyone talking about an opportunity. Do you chase or evaluate?

You feel confident after gains. Do you respect risk or ignore it?

You make a mistake. Do you spiral or reset?

These moments feel small.

They are not.

They define long-term outcomes.

## Common Athlete Mistakes and Financial Parallels

Athletes press after mistakes.

Financially, that leads to revenge trading and panic decisions.

Athletes follow momentum blindly.

Financially, that leads to herd behavior and buying high.

Athletes trust emotion over preparation.

Financially, that leads to regret and long-term damage.

The pattern is consistent.

The environment changes. Human behavior does not.

## Why Mastery Comes From Emotional Control

Markets do not reward brilliance.

They reward discipline.

They reward patience.

They reward restraint.

They reward consistency.

Talent helps. Knowledge helps. Emotional control decides.

If you can manage your emotions, you can manage your money. If you cannot, no strategy will save you.

## Reframing Success in the Mental Game

Success is not avoiding emotion.

It is responding correctly when emotion shows up.

Fear will appear.

Greed will appear.

Confidence will fluctuate.

That is normal.

The goal is not to eliminate emotion.

The goal is to prevent emotion from driving behavior.

## Winning the Long Game

The mental game separates winners from everyone else.

Not because winners feel less emotion, but because they have systems that protect them from themselves.

They reset faster.

They react less.

They trust preparation.

They play the next snap.

That is how championships are won.

That is how wealth is built.

## Athlete Takeaways

Fear, greed, and ego cost money.

Crowds are loud. Systems are quiet.

Discipline comes from structure, not willpower.

Chaos is part of the game.

Reset quickly and play the next snap.

Mental toughness compounds over time.

The next play is always coming.

How you respond determines everything.

# Part V: The Long Game (Taxes, Family, and Life Stages)

**Football ends. Life and money keep going.**

No matter how long you play, the season ends.

The schedule clears. The locker room empties. The structure that once defined your days fades away. What remains are the decisions you made along the way and the habits you carry forward.

Money does not stop when football does.

This part of the playbook focuses on what happens after the uniform comes off. Taxes. Careers. Housing. Retirement. Family responsibilities. Conversations that matter more with time.

These topics do not feel urgent early on. That is why they are often ignored. But just like conditioning, what you neglect early shows up later.

The long game is about positioning.

Positioning your money so taxes do not quietly erode it.

Positioning your career so income remains steady after sports.

Positioning your family so expectations are clear and conflict is minimized.

Positioning yourself so future decisions feel intentional, not forced.

This section is not about perfection. It is about awareness and preparation.

Football teaches you to think in seasons. Money requires you to think in decades. The decisions you make here determine whether life after football feels controlled or chaotic.

There are no crowds in this part of the game. No highlights. No applause.

Just responsibility.

Handled well, this phase brings freedom, flexibility, and confidence. Handled poorly, it creates pressure that never leaves.

Football ends.

The long game begins.

This section shows you how to play it.

# Chapter 19: Taxes and Where to Hold Your Money

Every player learns this lesson eventually.

You can gain ten yards on first down with a perfectly executed play. The line blocks. The receiver breaks free. Everything works. Then a flag comes out. Holding. False start. Illegal formation. The yards come right back. Sometimes more than that.

Penalties do not care how good the play was.

They only care about the rule that was broken.

Taxes work the same way.

You can invest well. You can earn more. You can make disciplined decisions over time. But if you ignore taxes, a meaningful portion of your progress quietly disappears. Not because you failed, but because you did not account for the rules of the game.

Taxes are not optional.

They are part of the game.

## Why Taxes Feel Invisible Until They Hurt

Most athletes are not taught to think about taxes early.

In sports, performance is measured in visible outcomes. Yards gained. Scores posted. Rankings achieved. Taxes operate differently. They are mechanical, delayed, and often invisible until after the fact. By the time they show up, the play is already over.

That delay creates confusion.

You feel like you are making progress. Your account balance grows. Your income increases. Then taxes reduce the result, sometimes dramatically. It feels like punishment, even though nothing went "wrong."

In reality, the rules were always there.

Understanding taxes is not about avoiding responsibility. It is about playing within the rules efficiently instead of giving away yardage unnecessarily.

## Taxable vs Tax-Advantaged Accounts

Not all accounts are treated the same.

Taxable accounts are the most straightforward. You invest, and taxes apply along the way. Interest income, dividends, and realized gains can create tax bills every year. These accounts offer flexibility, but they provide no built-in tax shelter.

Tax-advantaged accounts are designed with special rules.

They exist to encourage long-term behavior. Saving for retirement. Deferring consumption. Staying invested. In exchange for following the rules, you receive tax benefits.

In football terms, this is understanding the rulebook.

The same play can have different outcomes depending on where it is run. A legal formation in one situation becomes a penalty in another. The play did not change. The context did.

Where you hold your money matters just as much as how you invest it.

## Why Account Choice Is a Strategic Decision

Many people focus only on investment selection.

Which fund. Which stock. Which strategy.

That is like focusing only on play design without considering down, distance, and field position. Strategy is contextual. Taxes are part of that context.

Holding the same investment in different accounts can produce very different after-tax results. One account creates annual tax drag. Another allows growth to compound uninterrupted.

Over decades, that difference is enormous.

This is not about gaming the system.

It is about using the system as designed.

## Tax-Deferred Growth: Delaying the Penalty

Tax-deferred accounts allow you to postpone taxes until later.

You contribute money, often pre-tax. Investments grow without annual tax consequences. Taxes are paid when money is withdrawn. The benefit is compounding on the full amount instead of a reduced after-tax amount each year.

This can be powerful.

Deferring taxes allows more capital to stay invested longer. That extra growth compounds over time. For many people, deferral also aligns with lower income later in life, which can reduce the eventual tax cost.

In football terms, this is clock management.

Sometimes you slow the game down. You let time work in your favor. You protect the lead. Delaying taxes is a way of managing timing, not avoiding responsibility.

## Tax-Free Growth: Eliminating the Penalty Later

Tax-free accounts operate differently.

You pay taxes upfront, then invest. If the rules are followed, qualified withdrawals are not taxed at all. Growth, gains, and income come out clean.

This creates flexibility.

Tax-free accounts give you options later. They can be used strategically in years when income is higher. They can help manage tax brackets. They can provide spending power without triggering additional taxes.

In football terms, this is the two-minute drill.

You want flexibility. You want options. You want the ability to move without penalties. Tax-free growth gives you that later, at the cost of discipline earlier.

Both tax-deferred and tax-free accounts have roles.

The mistake is assuming one is always better than the other.

## Timing Matters More Than Most People Realize

Taxes are not just about rates.

They are about timing.

When income is earned.

When gains are realized.

When withdrawals happen.

Timing changes outcomes dramatically.

Two people with the same lifetime income can pay very different total taxes depending on when money is earned, invested, and withdrawn. Planning is not about predicting the future perfectly. It is about creating flexibility so you are not forced into bad timing.

In football terms, this is situational awareness.

You do not run the same play at the goal line as you do on your own twenty. Context matters. Timing matters.

## Asset Location: Putting Players in the Right Position

Asset location is deciding which investments go in which accounts.

Some investments create more taxes than others. Interest-heavy investments, high-turnover strategies, and income-generating assets tend to create ongoing tax bills. Growth-oriented investments often benefit more from long-term compounding.

Placing tax-heavy investments in tax-advantaged accounts reduces drag. Placing tax-efficient investments in taxable accounts preserves flexibility while minimizing penalties.

In football terms, this is personnel usage.

Even great players struggle when misused. A wide receiver does not belong on the line. A running back should not be asked to block every snap. Talent matters, but placement matters just as much.

Asset location sounds advanced, but the principle is simple.

Put things where they work best.

## Why Small Tax Mistakes Compound

One of the most dangerous aspects of taxes is that mistakes compound quietly.

An unnecessary annual tax bill reduces the amount that stays invested. That smaller base compounds to a smaller result. Over decades, the gap becomes massive.

This is rarely obvious year to year.

It shows up later, when balances are lower than expected and progress feels slower than it should.

In football terms, this is giving up small penalties repeatedly.

Five yards here. Ten yards there. No single mistake ends the game. But field position deteriorates. The margin for error shrinks. Eventually, you are playing from behind constantly.

Taxes work the same way.

## Common Tax Mistakes Athletes Make

Athletes make predictable tax mistakes, especially early in their careers.

Ignoring withholding and underestimating tax obligations.

Forgetting about quarterly taxes when income is irregular.

Selling investments without considering capital gains.

Assuming higher income automatically means higher wealth.

Failing to coordinate investments with tax planning.

These mistakes are not about intelligence.

They are about unfamiliarity with the system.

Taxes are mechanical. They follow rules, not emotions. Misunderstanding them creates frustration because the outcome feels unfair, even though it was predictable.

## Why Taxes Feel Like They Undo Progress

Taxes feel different than expenses.

Expenses are choices. Taxes feel imposed. That emotional difference causes people to avoid thinking about them. Avoidance makes outcomes worse.

Athletes understand this dynamic intuitively.

Penalties feel worse than missed opportunities because they take something away. But penalties are preventable. They are about discipline and awareness.

Taxes are similar.

You cannot eliminate them entirely, but you can minimize unnecessary ones through planning.

## Planning for Taxes Is Part of Discipline

Ignoring taxes does not make them go away.

It just makes them show up later, often at the worst possible time.

Planning for taxes is not pessimistic. It is disciplined. It is acknowledging that rules exist and choosing to operate within them efficiently.

In football terms, this is protecting field position.

You may not score on every drive, but you do not give yards away for free. You play clean. You make the opponent earn it.

## Coach's Perspective on Taxes

A coach would not sugarcoat this.

Know the rules.

Protect field position.

Do not give yards away.

Play smart.

Penalties are frustrating because they are avoidable. Taxes often are too.

Awareness does not eliminate responsibility.

It reduces unnecessary damage.

## Game Situations and Decision Points

Tax discipline shows up in quiet decisions.

You earn more. Do you plan for taxes or react later?

You sell an investment. Do you understand the tax impact?

You choose an account. Do you think long term or short term?

You receive a windfall. Do you protect it or leak it away?

Same decisions.

Same discipline.

The best outcomes come from thinking ahead, not scrambling afterward.

## Why Taxes Should Be Integrated, Not Isolated

One of the biggest mistakes people make is treating taxes as a separate topic.

Investing decisions affect taxes.

Saving decisions affect taxes.

Spending decisions affect taxes.

Career decisions affect taxes.

Everything is connected.

In sports terms, special teams still matter. Offense and defense do not operate in isolation. Field position connects everything.

Taxes are the connective tissue of financial decisions.

Ignoring them weakens the entire system.

## Winning the Long Game

Taxes will always be part of the game.

You cannot avoid them. You cannot outwork them. You cannot ignore them. But you can respect them.

Smart players learn how to minimize mistakes, manage timing, and keep more of what they earn over time. They play clean. They protect yardage. They let discipline compound.

The goal is not to eliminate taxes.

The goal is to stop giving progress back unnecessarily.

## Athlete Takeaways

Taxes affect every investment decision.

Where you hold money matters.

Timing changes outcomes.

Small tax mistakes compound over time.

Discipline applies off the field too.

Know the rules and protect yardage.

You would never accept penalties every drive and expect to win.

Treat taxes the same way.

Play smart.

# Chapter 20: Retirement Accounts and Financial Independence

Every player thinks about the end of the season.

Not because they want it to end, but because they plan for it. Strength programs evolve. Recovery becomes a priority. Reps are managed differently. Coaches stop asking one player to carry everything because they know the real goal is not one game. It is making it through the entire year healthy, effective, and ready.

Retirement planning works the same way.

It is not about stopping work. It is not about being old. It is not about checking out of life. It is about building options. Freedom. Control over your time, energy, and choices.

Financial independence is the long season after football.

And like any long season, it rewards preparation, pacing, and consistency far more than intensity or last-minute effort.

## Why Retirement Planning Feels Abstract to Athletes

For athletes, time is structured in short windows.

Seasons. Games. Practices. Cycles. Everything has a start date and an end date. Retirement planning does not fit neatly into that framework. It feels distant, vague, and optional. There is no scoreboard. No urgency. No visible consequence for delaying.

That is why many athletes postpone it.

The problem is that retirement planning is not about age. It is about time in the system. Compounding does not care how old you are. It only cares how long money is allowed to work.

Waiting does not feel like a mistake in the moment. It feels reasonable. The cost shows up decades later, when options are fewer and pressure is higher.

## Retirement Planning Is About Options, Not Quitting

One of the biggest misconceptions is that retirement planning is about never working again.

For most people, it is not.

It is about choice.

The choice to work less.

The choice to change careers.

The choice to take time off.

The choice to say no to bad situations.

In football terms, this is depth.

Depth does not mean the starter quits. It means the team has options. It means injuries do not end the season. It means flexibility exists when conditions change.

Financial independence creates depth in your life.

## 401(k)s and Employer Plans: The First Line of the Game Plan

Employer retirement plans are often the first real investing opportunity most people get.

401(k)s allow you to contribute automatically from each paycheck. Money moves before you see it. That matters. Discipline is built into the system. Many employers also offer matching contributions.

That match is free money.

In football terms, this is taking what the defense gives you.

If an employer matches part of your contribution and you do not participate, you are leaving points on the field. There is no upside to skipping a match. It is one of the few guaranteed returns available.

These plans matter not because they are exciting, but because they are automatic.

Automation beats intention every time.

You do not rely on motivation. You do not have to remember. You do not negotiate with yourself. The system does the work.

## Why Automatic Contributions Are So Powerful

Automatic contributions solve the hardest problem in retirement planning.

Consistency.

Most people fail not because they choose bad investments, but because they contribute irregularly or stop altogether. Automation removes that friction.

In sports terms, this is conditioning.

You do not get in shape by training only when you feel like it. You get in shape by following a schedule. Automatic contributions create financial conditioning.

Over time, the habit becomes invisible, and progress accumulates quietly.

## Traditional and Roth IRAs: Different Tools, Different Purposes

Beyond employer plans, individual retirement accounts add flexibility.

Traditional IRAs provide tax-deferred growth. Contributions may reduce current taxable income. Taxes are paid later when money is withdrawn.

Roth IRAs work differently. Contributions are made with after-tax money. Qualified withdrawals are tax-free. Growth comes out clean.

Both serve important roles.

Traditional accounts help manage taxes now.

Roth accounts create flexibility later.

In football terms, this is balancing run and pass.

You do not commit to one exclusively. You adjust based on situation, field position, and opponent. The same is true with retirement accounts.

The mistake is assuming one is always better.

The better question is, what role does this account play in my long-term plan?

## Why Flexibility Later Matters More Than You Think

Taxes do not disappear in retirement.

Income sources shift, but tax planning remains critical. Having money in different types of accounts allows you to manage withdrawals strategically. That flexibility reduces lifetime taxes and increases control.

In football terms, this is play-calling flexibility.

If you only have one option, defenses adjust. If you have multiple options, you dictate tempo. Tax flexibility lets you adapt instead of react.

Roth accounts are not just about tax savings. They are about control.

## Contribution and Withdrawal Rules: Know the Rulebook

Retirement accounts come with rules.

Contribution limits.

Income limits.

Withdrawal restrictions.

Early withdrawal penalties.

These rules are not arbitrary. They exist to encourage long-term behavior and discourage short-term misuse.

In football terms, this is staying onside.

You can run a great play, but if you line up incorrectly, it comes back. Knowing the rules does not limit performance. It protects it.

Understanding contribution limits prevents missed opportunities. Understanding withdrawal rules prevents penalties that undo years of progress.

Ignorance is expensive here.

## Why Early Withdrawals Hurt More Than They Appear

Pulling money out of retirement accounts early often feels necessary in the moment.

Life happens. Emergencies arise. But early withdrawals usually come with penalties and taxes that permanently reduce future potential.

In football terms, this is sacrificing long-term field position for a short-term gain.

Sometimes it is unavoidable. Often it is the result of poor planning elsewhere. Emergency funds and proper savings exist to protect retirement assets from being used prematurely.

Protecting retirement money matters because time cannot be replaced.

## Retirement Income Basics: Saving Is Only Half the Game

Saving for retirement is not the finish line.

Eventually, money needs to produce income. Withdrawals must be planned. Taxes matter. Sequence matters. Timing matters.

Many people focus exclusively on accumulation and never think about distribution. That creates problems later.

In football terms, this is moving the ball but not finishing drives.

Yardage without points does not win games. Savings without a withdrawal plan creates uncertainty and stress.

Planning for income turns a pile of assets into a sustainable system.

## The Sequence Problem

One of the least understood risks in retirement is sequence risk.

The order in which returns occur matters when withdrawals begin. Poor timing early in retirement can have an outsized impact, even if long-term averages look fine.

This is why planning matters.

In football terms, this is game flow.

The same plays produce different outcomes depending on when they are run. Strategy must account for timing, not just totals.

## Why Athletes Underestimate Longevity

Athletes are used to short careers and defined timelines.

That mindset does not translate well to retirement planning. People often underestimate how long retirement can last. Thirty years or more is common.

That requires endurance, not sprinting.

In football terms, this is conditioning for overtime.

You do not train only for regulation and hope it works out. You plan for the long haul.

## Coach's Perspective on Retirement Planning

A coach would frame it clearly.

Plan ahead.

Take the free yards.

Stay disciplined.

Finish strong.

No coach builds a season plan around last-minute heroics. Championships are won through preparation and consistency.

Retirement planning rewards the same traits.

## Game Situations and Decision Points

These decisions seem small in isolation.

You have access to an employer plan. Do you contribute or delay?

You choose between Traditional and Roth. Do you understand the trade-offs?

You change jobs. Do you roll accounts thoughtfully or forget them?

You earn more. Do you increase contributions or inflate lifestyle?

Each decision compounds over time.

There is no whistle when you make the wrong choice. The impact shows up later.

## Common Athlete Mistakes and Financial Parallels

Athletes focus on the present.

Financially, that delays retirement planning.

Athletes underestimate longevity.

Financially, that creates shortfalls.

Athletes wait too long to adjust training.

Financially, that limits options.

The pattern is consistent.

## Why Consistency Beats Catch-Up

Many people tell themselves they will save more later.

That logic rarely works.

Life gets more complex, not less. Responsibilities increase. Expenses grow. Time shrinks. Catch-up is harder than starting early and staying steady.

In football terms, this is trying to win a season with one great game.

It does not work.

## Financial Independence as a Phase, Not an Event

Financial independence is not a finish line you cross one day.

It is a gradual shift.

Less pressure.

More flexibility.

More control.

It happens slowly, almost invisibly, until one day you realize options exist that did not before.

That is the goal.

## Winning the Long Game

Financial independence is built slowly.

Reps matter.

Time matters.

Discipline matters.

You do not sprint through a marathon season. You pace it. You manage energy. You stay consistent even when progress feels boring.

That is how long seasons are won.

## Athlete Takeaways

Retirement planning is about options, not quitting.

Employer matches are free points.

Automation creates discipline.

Traditional and Roth accounts serve different purposes.

Rules matter. Know them.

Income planning is as important as saving.

Independence comes from consistency over time.

The season does not end when the clock hits zero.

It changes.

And the players who planned for that change are the ones who stay in control.

# Chapter 21: Housing and Big Financial Decisions

Every coach talks about situational awareness.

Field position.

Time on the clock.

Score.

Personnel on the field.

A play that makes sense in one situation is a disaster in another. Throwing deep on third and short near midfield is different than doing it backed up on your own goal line. Great players do not just know the playbook. They understand context before they act.

Big financial decisions work the same way.

Housing, cars, and major purchases are not just about what you want. They are about timing, flexibility, risk, and long-term consequences. When context is ignored, even "reasonable" decisions can create years of stress. When context is respected, progress feels controlled instead of forced.

This chapter is about learning to read the situation before committing to big moves.

## Why Big Purchases Feel Heavier Than Expected

Athletes are used to big moments.

Games. Competitions. Decisions under pressure. But financial decisions hit differently. There is no clock. No coach calling timeout. No clear right answer in the moment. The consequences unfold slowly, often long after the excitement fades.

That delay makes mistakes harder to recognize.

A purchase can feel good today and quietly limit options for years. That is why situational awareness matters more with big financial decisions than almost any other area.

## Renting vs Buying: Flexibility vs Commitment

Renting and buying are not moral choices. They are strategic ones.

Renting provides flexibility.

Buying creates commitment.

Renting allows you to move easily. It limits responsibility for repairs and maintenance. Upfront costs are lower. Cash flow is more predictable. You can adapt quickly if life changes.

Buying builds equity over time. It provides stability. It locks in housing costs over the long run. It can be a powerful wealth-building tool when timing and circumstances align.

In football terms, renting is playing on a short-term contract.

You have mobility. You can change teams. You can respond to opportunity without being tied down.

Buying is signing a long-term deal.

It can be great if you know the system, trust the organization, and plan to stay. It can be limiting if circumstances change unexpectedly.

Neither option is better by default.

The right choice depends on income stability, career stage, location, family plans, and how long you realistically expect to stay in one place.

Buying too early can trap you.

Waiting too long can slow progress.

Context matters.

## Why Buying Too Early Can Create Pressure

Buying a home too early is one of the most common mistakes former athletes make.

Not because buying is bad, but because timing is ignored.

When income is unstable, careers are still evolving, or location is uncertain, buying reduces flexibility. Selling is expensive. Moving is harder. Stress increases when life changes but housing cannot adjust.

In football terms, this is committing to a long-term play without knowing the roster.

You might like the idea of stability, but if the situation changes, the commitment becomes a burden.

Renting during uncertain seasons is not failure.

It is discipline.

## Mortgages and Down Payments: Understanding Leverage

A mortgage is long-term leverage.

It allows you to control a large asset with a smaller upfront investment. That leverage can work in your favor over time, but it also magnifies mistakes.

Mortgages do not just represent a monthly payment. They represent decades of obligation. Taxes. Insurance. Maintenance. Repairs. Opportunity cost.

Down payments matter because they reduce risk.

A larger down payment lowers monthly payments. It provides margin if values fluctuate. It gives flexibility if life changes. It reduces stress during uncertain periods.

In football terms, leverage is aggression.

Used correctly, it moves the ball.

Used poorly, it creates turnovers.

Just because a lender approves you for a large mortgage does not mean it fits your situation. Approval is not readiness. It is simply capacity under a formula.

Understand what you are committing to before you sign.

## The Hidden Costs of Homeownership

Many people underestimate the true cost of owning a home.

Mortgage payments are only part of the picture.

Maintenance. Repairs. Property taxes. Insurance. Utilities. Time. Mental energy.

None of these show up clearly at closing. They show up later, often unexpectedly.

In football terms, this is ignoring special teams.

Offense and defense matter, but hidden costs still decide field position. Ignoring them creates surprises that change outcomes.

Homeownership can be a great tool. It just needs to be entered intentionally.

## Cars, Leases, and Financing Traps

Cars are one of the most common financial mistakes athletes make.

They are emotional purchases. They are visible. They signal success. They feel earned. And they depreciate the moment you drive them off the lot.

Cars lose value.

They require insurance.

They require maintenance.

They tie up cash flow.

Leases feel affordable because payments are lower. Loans feel manageable because terms are long. Both can trap cash flow if chosen without context.

In football terms, this is choosing flash over fundamentals.

The play looks good. The crowd reacts. But the cost shows up later when the drive stalls.

Transportation should support your life, not strain it.

A reliable, reasonable car creates freedom. An expensive one creates obligation.

## Why Monthly Payments Are a Trap

One of the most dangerous ways to evaluate purchases is by monthly payment alone.

Longer terms make expensive items feel affordable. Lower payments hide the true cost. Interest compounds quietly. Cash flow gets squeezed.

In football terms, this is focusing on one down instead of the entire drive.

You may convert now, but you sacrifice future flexibility. Good situational awareness looks beyond the next snap.

Ask better questions.

How does this payment affect my ability to save?

How long am I committing?

What happens if income changes?

What opportunities does this limit?

Those questions matter more than whether you can "afford" the payment today.

## Planning Large Purchases Instead of Reacting to Them

Big purchases should never be surprises.

Homes. Vehicles. Weddings. Education. Business investments. These events are predictable. They may not have exact dates, but they are not random.

Planning ahead changes everything.

Saving in advance reduces stress.

Borrowing less preserves flexibility.

Timing becomes intentional instead of reactive.

In football terms, this is knowing the play before the snap.

You do not improvise on fourth down. You prepare. You understand the situation. You commit with confidence.

Reactive purchases feel exciting. They often lead to regret.

Planned purchases create control.

## The Cost of Emotional Buying

Emotional buying feels justified in the moment.

You worked hard. You deserve it. Others have it. You do not want to miss out.

Emotion overrides context.

In sports terms, this is forcing the ball when coverage is tight. You want the big play, even though the situation does not call for it.

Emotional purchases often come with long-term consequences that far outlast the emotion that drove them.

Situational awareness prevents this.

## Flexibility as a Competitive Advantage

One of the most underrated assets in personal finance is flexibility.

The ability to move.

The ability to change direction.

The ability to say no.

Big fixed commitments reduce flexibility. That does not mean they are wrong. It means they should be chosen carefully.

In football terms, flexibility is play-calling freedom.

When you are not boxed in, you can adapt. When you are overcommitted, your options shrink.

Good financial decisions preserve flexibility whenever possible.

## Coach's Perspective on Big Decisions

A coach would say it plainly.

Know the situation.

Do not force it.

Think long term.

Protect flexibility.

Great coaches care less about winning one play and more about managing the entire game. Big financial decisions deserve the same patience and awareness.

## Game Situations and Decision Points

Situational awareness shows up in quiet moments.

You feel pressure to buy. Do you check readiness or react emotionally?

You qualify for more than you expected. Do you spend the max or stay disciplined?

You want something now. Do you plan for it or finance it impulsively?

Your life changes. Do you reassess commitments or ignore them?

These moments define financial seasons.

## Common Athlete Mistakes and Financial Parallels

Athletes rush commitments.

Financially, that means buying too early.

Athletes confuse approval with readiness.

Financially, that means over-borrowing.

Athletes chase image.

Financially, that leads to cash flow stress.

The pattern is consistent.

When context is ignored, discipline breaks down.

## Redefining "Affordability"

Affordability is not about whether you can make the payment.

It is about whether the decision supports your life, goals, and flexibility over time.

If a purchase limits saving, increases stress, or reduces options, it may be affordable on paper and costly in reality.

Athletes understand this intuitively in sports.

A play can work and still be the wrong call.

## Winning the Long Game

Housing and major purchases should support your life, not control it.

The best decisions create stability, flexibility, and confidence. They allow progress to continue without constant pressure. They fit the season you are in instead of forcing you into one you are not ready for.

Situational awareness separates good decisions from costly ones.

## Athlete Takeaways

Big financial decisions require context, not emotion.

Renting and buying serve different seasons of life.

Mortgages are long-term commitments. Respect them.

Cars lose value. Keep them in perspective.

Monthly payments hide true costs.

Plan large purchases before they happen.

Flexibility is an asset. Protect it.

In sports, situational awareness wins games.

In life, it protects options.

Read the field before you commit.

# Chapter 22: Your Career Is Your Greatest Asset

Every player eventually learns this truth.

Your career is more than one game. More than one season. More than one contract. It is a body of work built over time. Coaches manage reps because overuse shortens careers. Strength staffs manage load because durability matters. Veterans understand that longevity beats one highlight play that costs you the rest of the year.

Your career after football works the same way.

Income is not just what you make this year. It is the engine that funds every other financial goal. Saving, investing, flexibility, and security all depend on the strength and sustainability of that engine. When income is unstable or mismanaged, everything else becomes harder. When it is developed intentionally, options expand.

This chapter is about treating your career like the long season it is.

## Why Athletes Underestimate Career Impact

Athletes are trained to focus on performance in the moment.

Next game. Next season. Next role. That mindset is necessary in sports, but it can be limiting in career decisions after football. Jobs are often evaluated based on immediate pay, title, or prestige, rather than long-term development and sustainability.

That short-term lens creates problems.

Income feels like a score for the year instead of a system that compounds over decades. Career decisions are made emotionally instead of strategically. Opportunities are chased without considering fit, growth, or cost.

Your career is not a sprint.

It is an endurance event with changing terrain.

## Salary vs Total Compensation

Salary is only part of the picture.

Benefits, bonuses, retirement matches, health insurance, disability coverage, time off, flexibility, and growth opportunities all matter. Two jobs with the same salary can produce very different outcomes over time.

In football terms, salary is base pay.

Total compensation is the full contract.

The full contract includes guarantees, incentives, benefits, and long-term security. Focusing only on base pay misses the bigger picture.

Examples of compensation elements that matter:

- Employer retirement contributions
- Health insurance premiums and deductibles
- Disability and life insurance
- Paid time off and flexibility
- Bonuses and performance incentives
- Tuition assistance or professional development
- Vesting schedules and long-term benefits

A job with slightly lower salary but strong benefits can outperform a higher-paying job with weak support. Over time, those differences compound.

Understanding total compensation helps you make decisions that support your life, not just your ego.

## Why Benefits Matter More Than You Think

Benefits are easy to ignore because they are not always visible.

You feel salary immediately. Benefits work quietly. That makes them easy to undervalue. Until you need them.

Health insurance matters when something unexpected happens. Disability insurance matters if income stops. Retirement matches matter decades later when compounding has had time to work.

In football terms, this is depth and conditioning.

You may not notice them every snap, but when something goes wrong, they determine whether the season continues or collapses.

Ignoring benefits is not confidence.

It is incomplete evaluation.

## Job Changes and Career Transitions

Changing jobs affects more than income.

Health insurance resets. Retirement plans change. Vesting schedules may restart. Time off policies differ. Culture and expectations shift. Career trajectory can accelerate or stall depending on the move.

In football terms, this is switching teams.

You are not just changing uniforms. You are learning a new system, earning trust, understanding the locker room, and adapting to different expectations. Talent alone is not enough. Fit matters.

Common transition mistakes include:

- Focusing only on salary
- Overlooking vesting or benefit loss
- Underestimating cultural mismatch
- Ignoring workload and burnout risk
- Failing to plan for insurance gaps

Career moves should be evaluated holistically. The best move is not always the highest-paying one. It is the one that supports growth, stability, and sustainability.

## Negotiation Basics

Negotiation is not confrontation.

It is communication.

Many former athletes avoid negotiation because it feels uncomfortable. They worry about appearing greedy, ungrateful, or difficult. Others overcompensate and become aggressive without preparation.

Neither approach works.

Effective negotiation starts with understanding your value and the role. It requires preparation, not emotion. It is about alignment, not winning.

In football terms, this is contract negotiation.

Players who understand their role, market value, and leverage negotiate better outcomes. Players who rely on emotion or entitlement often misjudge the situation.

Good negotiation focuses on:

- Market research
- Role expectations
- Performance metrics
- Long-term growth opportunities
- Benefits and flexibility, not just pay

You do not need to demand everything.

You need to ask informed questions and advocate professionally.

Negotiation shapes income, benefits, workload, and career trajectory. Avoiding it leaves value on the table.

## Timing Matters in Negotiation

Negotiation is not a one-time event.

Timing matters.

Early in a role, your leverage may be limited. As you demonstrate value, leverage increases. Preparing for future negotiations is part of career management.

In football terms, this is playing yourself into a better contract.

You earn leverage through performance, reliability, and fit. Planning ahead allows you to negotiate from strength instead of desperation.

## Side Income and Entrepreneurship

Side income can create flexibility and resilience.

Consulting. Coaching. Speaking. Content creation. Small businesses. NIL-related opportunities. These can supplement primary income and reduce dependence on one employer.

In football terms, this is cross-training.

It builds resilience. If one area slows down, another can carry the load. Side income can also evolve into a primary career over time if it aligns with skills and interests.

However, not every opportunity is worth chasing.

Side income requires discipline. Time, energy, and focus are limited. Chasing every opportunity leads to burnout and diluted effort.

Good side income decisions:

- Align with skills and interests
- Do not jeopardize primary income
- Have clear boundaries
- Support long-term goals

Side income should add flexibility, not chaos.

## Why Burnout Is a Career Risk

Athletes understand overtraining.

Too many reps without recovery leads to injury. Careers after football have similar risks. Overworking, under-recovering, and chasing every opportunity erodes performance over time.

Burnout reduces income potential, creativity, and health. It often appears after periods of success, not failure.

Managing workload is not weakness.

It is strategy.

## Career Longevity Requires Intentional Management

Your career is your biggest financial asset.

It funds savings. It funds investing. It funds lifestyle. It funds security. No portfolio works without income behind it.

That means your career deserves the same discipline you applied to training.

That includes:

- Skill development
- Network building
- Reputation management
- Health and energy management
- Long-term planning

Ignoring career management creates fragile income. Managing it intentionally creates options.

## Coach's Perspective on Career Management

A coach would frame it simply.

Take care of your body.

Take care of your career.

Think long term.

Know your worth.

No coach builds a program around burning out star players. Sustainable success requires pacing, development, and recovery.

Your career deserves the same respect.

## Game Situations and Decision Points

Career discipline shows up in quiet decisions.

You receive a job offer. Do you evaluate the whole package or just salary?

You feel underpaid. Do you prepare for negotiation or complain silently?

You see a side opportunity. Do you assess fit or chase excitement?

You feel burned out. Do you adjust or push harder?

These moments compound.

There is no scoreboard, but outcomes reveal the pattern.

## Common Athlete Mistakes and Financial Parallels

Athletes focus on short-term roles.

Financially, that limits long-term growth.

Athletes ignore benefits and recovery.

Financially, that creates gaps and stress.

Athletes chase every opportunity.

Financially, that leads to burnout and inconsistency.

The pattern is familiar.

Short-term intensity without long-term planning eventually breaks.

## Redefining Career Success

Career success is not just income growth.

It is income sustainability.

It is flexibility.

It is alignment with values.

It is health and energy over time.

In football terms, this is making it through the season strong, not just starting hot.

You do not need to win every contract negotiation.

You need to build a career that lasts.

## Winning the Long Game

Your career is your biggest asset because it funds everything else.

Protect it.

Develop it.

Negotiate thoughtfully.

Manage transitions intentionally.

Add side income strategically.

Treat your career with the same discipline you brought to football. Plan for longevity. Respect recovery. Focus on consistency.

Highlights fade.

Sustainable careers compound.

## Athlete Takeaways

Your career is a long season, not one game.

Salary is only part of the picture.

Benefits and flexibility matter more than people realize.

Negotiation is preparation, not confrontation.

Side income creates resilience when done intentionally.

Burnout is a real risk. Manage load.

Longevity beats short-term wins.

You trained for years to perform on the field.

Bring that same discipline to your career, and it will support you for decades.

# Chapter 23: Estate Planning Basics for Every Player

Every team has an emergency plan.

If the quarterback goes down, someone steps in. If communication breaks, there is a backup system. If chaos hits, roles are already defined. No one waits until the moment of crisis to decide who does what. Preparation happens long before it is needed.

Estate planning is that same preparation for life.

It is not about expecting something bad to happen. It is about making sure decisions are made the way you want them made if you cannot make them yourself. Avoiding this conversation does not avoid the outcome. It only hands control to the wrong people at the worst possible time.

This chapter is about leadership, responsibility, and clarity when pressure is highest.

## Why Estate Planning Feels Easy to Postpone

Estate planning feels uncomfortable because it forces people to confront things they would rather avoid.

Loss.

Incapacity.

Family conflict.

Hard conversations.

For athletes especially, estate planning often feels premature. You are healthy. You are capable. Life feels open-ended. Planning for worst-case scenarios feels unnecessary, even pessimistic.

But that mindset misunderstands what estate planning actually is.

Estate planning is not about death.

It is about decision-making.

In sports terms, this is not planning for failure. It is planning for contingencies. You do not expect injuries, but you prepare for them anyway. You do not expect communication breakdowns, but you have backups. You do not expect chaos, but you train for it.

Preparation is not pessimism.

It is professionalism.

## What Happens When You Do Nothing

When there is no estate plan, decisions still get made.

They are just made by default rules.

State laws decide who receives assets. Courts decide who manages money. Judges decide who handles guardianship. Doctors and institutions make healthcare decisions without guidance. Families guess. Stress multiplies. Conflict increases.

This is not rare.

Most estate disasters are not caused by complex wealth. They are caused by lack of clarity.

In football terms, this is snapping the ball with no play call. Everyone moves, but no one is aligned. Chaos follows.

Doing nothing is not neutral.

It is a decision to let others decide for you.

## Wills: The Base Playbook

A will is a set of instructions.

It explains:

- Who receives your assets
- Who is responsible for carrying out your wishes
- Who will care for minor children
- How things should be handled after you are gone

Without a will, the state decides all of this.

That means laws, not relationships, determine outcomes.

In football terms, a will is the base playbook.

It sets structure. It assigns roles. It removes guesswork. It does not have to be complicated to be effective. It just has to exist and reflect your intentions.

A simple will is far better than no will.

Perfection is not required. Clarity is.

## Trusts: Advanced Packages, Not Default Requirements

Trusts add another layer of control.

They can:

- Manage how and when assets are distributed
- Protect beneficiaries who are young or financially inexperienced
- Provide privacy
- Reduce administrative complications
- Address complex family situations

Not everyone needs a trust.

That is important.

In football terms, a trust is an advanced package. You do not install it unless it fits your personnel and situation. Adding complexity for its own sake creates confusion.

The mistake is thinking estate planning must be complicated to be effective.

It does not.

You start with the basics and add tools only when they serve a purpose.

## Beneficiaries: The Most Overlooked Detail

Beneficiaries override almost everything.

Retirement accounts.

Life insurance policies.

Many investment accounts.

These assets pass based on beneficiary designations, not what your will says.

That means your estate plan can look perfect on paper and still fail completely if beneficiaries are outdated or incorrect.

Common problems include:

- An ex-spouse still listed as beneficiary
- A parent named decades ago who can no longer serve
- Missing contingent beneficiaries
- Accounts that were never updated after marriage or children

In football terms, this is assignment clarity.

You can have a great play drawn up, but if players line up incorrectly, the play fails. Beneficiaries are assignments. If they are wrong, nothing works as intended.

One outdated beneficiary can undo years of planning.

Reviewing beneficiaries is one of the simplest and most impactful steps you can take. It is also one of the most commonly ignored.

## Account Titling: Ownership Determines Control

How assets are titled matters.

Individual ownership.

Joint ownership.

Payable-on-death designations.

Trust ownership.

Each structure changes who controls assets, how they pass, and what happens during incapacity or death.

Many people accumulate accounts over time without ever reviewing how they are titled. That creates fragmentation and confusion.

In football terms, this is role confusion.

If no one knows who has authority, execution breaks down under pressure. Account titling defines authority.

Consistency matters. Alignment matters.

## Powers of Attorney: Protection While You Are Alive

Estate planning is not only about death.

It is also about incapacity.

A power of attorney allows someone you trust to act on your behalf if you cannot. This includes paying bills, managing accounts, signing documents, and handling financial obligations.

Without a power of attorney, loved ones may be locked out of helping you when help is most needed. Courts may need to get involved. Delays happen. Stress increases.

In football terms, this is naming a captain.

When you are not available, someone has authority. Roles are clear. Action is possible.

There are typically two key forms:

- Financial power of attorney
- Medical power of attorney

Both matter.

Choosing the right person matters more than choosing the perfect document. Trust and communication are essential.

## Healthcare Directives: Reducing Stress When Stakes Are High

Healthcare directives outline your wishes for medical care.

They guide decisions if you cannot speak for yourself. They also protect loved ones from having to guess under emotional pressure.

This is not about controlling every detail.

It is about providing guidance.

In football terms, this is communication under pressure.

When the game is tight and emotions are high, clarity matters most. Healthcare directives remove uncertainty at the worst possible moments.

They reduce:

- Family conflict
- Emotional burden
- Confusion during crises

They protect your autonomy and your family.

## Why Estate Planning Is Really About People

Estate planning is often framed as a financial exercise.

In reality, it is relational.

It protects:

- Spouses
- Children
- Parents
- Siblings
- Partners
- Anyone who depends on you or is affected by your decisions

Clear plans prevent arguments. They reduce resentment. They allow loved ones to focus on healing instead of logistics.

In football terms, this is protecting the team.

You plan so others do not have to scramble when pressure is high.

The goal is not control.

The goal is care.

## Common Estate Planning Mistakes Athletes Make

Patterns show up repeatedly.

Avoiding uncomfortable conversations.

Delaying because everything feels fine.

Assuming family will "figure it out."

Creating documents once and never updating them.

Overcomplicating or completely avoiding the process.

These mistakes are not about intelligence.

They are about discomfort.

Preparation reduces discomfort later. Avoidance transfers it to others.

## Estate Planning Is Not One-and-Done

Estate planning is a process, not an event.

Life changes require updates:

- Marriage
- Divorce
- Children
- Career changes
- Moves
- Health changes
- Asset growth

In football terms, this is updating the playbook as the roster changes.

You do not run the same scheme forever without adjustment. Reviewing documents does not mean something is wrong. It means you are paying attention.

Periodic reviews keep plans aligned with reality.

## Coach's Perspective on Estate Planning

A coach would not dance around this.

Handle your business.

Protect the team.

Do not leave things unclear.

Be responsible.

No coach waits for an emergency to assign roles.

Estate planning is leadership beyond the field.

## Game Situations and Decision Points

Estate planning decisions are quiet.

You think you are too young. Do you prepare anyway?

Your life changes. Do you update documents or ignore them?

You assume loved ones know your wishes. Do you confirm or hope?

You feel uncomfortable. Do you act anyway?

These moments do not feel urgent.

Their consequences are.

## Why Preparation Is a Gift, Not a Burden

The people you care about will never thank you in advance for estate planning.

They will thank you later through reduced stress, fewer conflicts, and clearer outcomes.

Estate planning is one of the most generous things you can do for others because it removes uncertainty when they are least equipped to handle it.

That is leadership.

## Winning the Long Game

Estate planning is not about wealth.

It is about clarity, control, and care.

You do this so decisions are made the right way. So people are protected. So chaos is minimized. So leadership continues even when you cannot step in.

Just like sports, preparation behind the scenes determines performance under pressure.

## Athlete Takeaways

Estate planning is about responsibility, not fear.

A will gives direction. Without it, the state decides.

Trusts add control when appropriate, not by default.

Beneficiaries override almost everything. Review them.

Account titling determines control.

Powers of attorney protect you while you are alive.

Healthcare directives reduce stress and conflict.

Estate planning is not one-and-done. Review it as life changes.

Preparation is an act of leadership.

Every team has an emergency plan.

Your life deserves one too.

# Chapter 24: Talking About Money With Family

Every successful team communicates.

On the field. In the locker room. In meetings. During film review. Communication is constant because assignments matter. When communication breaks down, talent cannot fix confusion. Missed assignments lead to blown coverages. Assumptions create frustration. Silence turns small issues into big problems.

Money works the same way inside families.

Most financial problems between family members do not start with money itself. They start with silence, assumptions, unspoken expectations, and avoided conversations. When communication is missing, even good intentions can create lasting damage.

This chapter is about building clear, healthy communication around money so families function like strong teams instead of disconnected individuals.

## Why Money Is Hard to Talk About in Families

Money carries emotion.

Fear. Pride. Guilt. Control. Shame. Comparison. Expectations passed down over generations. Unlike sports, there is no universal rulebook for family finances. Every household brings its own history and assumptions.

That makes money conversations feel risky.

People avoid them to protect peace in the short term. Unfortunately, avoidance usually does the opposite in the long term. Silence creates misunderstandings. Misunderstandings become resentment. Resentment damages relationships.

In sports terms, this is ignoring a coverage breakdown because no one wants to call it out. The problem does not disappear. It shows up later in a big way.

Communication is not about control.

It is about clarity.

## Teaching Kids About Money: Modeling Beats Lecturing

Kids learn by watching, not by listening.

You can tell kids to save, but if they see impulsive spending, they learn impulse. You can talk about budgeting, but if money is always a source of stress or secrecy, they learn avoidance.

In football terms, this is fundamentals.

You do not teach young players advanced schemes first. You teach stance, effort, responsibility, and awareness. Money is the same.

Simple lessons early matter more than complex strategies later.

Examples of early money fundamentals:

- Explaining needs vs wants
- Letting kids handle small amounts of money
- Showing how saving works over time
- Talking openly about trade-offs
- Connecting work to earning

These lessons build confidence and familiarity. Money stops feeling mysterious or taboo. Kids learn that money is a tool, not a source of fear.

## Allowances, Chores, and Responsibility

Families differ on allowances, but the principle matters more than the structure.

Kids benefit from understanding:

- Money is finite
- Choices have consequences
- Saving requires patience
- Spending is intentional

In sports terms, this is accountability.

You earn reps by showing up. You earn trust through responsibility. Whether money is tied to chores, goals, or allowances, the key is consistency and clarity.

Avoid using money as a constant reward or punishment. That creates emotional associations that are hard to break later. Focus on teaching decision-making instead of control.

## Talking to Teenagers About Real Money Decisions

Teenagers are closer to real-world consequences.

Jobs. Cars. Insurance. Phones. Spending habits. Peer pressure increases. Conversations matter more here because habits are forming fast.

In football terms, this is skill development before varsity play.

Mistakes now are cheaper than mistakes later. Teaching how credit works, how interest accumulates, and how budgeting actually feels prepares them for independence.

Avoid scare tactics.

Education works better than fear.

## College Students and Young Adults: Coaching Before Mistakes

Young adults face real money decisions quickly.

Credit cards. Student loans. Rent. First jobs. Benefits. Taxes. NIL income for athletes. Without guidance, mistakes compound fast.

In football terms, this is a freshman learning the system.

Clear coaching prevents costly errors. Silence forces them to learn through pain.

Key conversations to have early:

- How credit cards actually work
- The long-term cost of debt
- How to read a paycheck
- How taxes reduce income
- Why saving early matters
- How lifestyle choices affect cash flow

These conversations do not have to be lectures.

They should be ongoing, practical, and judgment-free.

The goal is not perfection.

It is awareness.

## NIL, Windfalls, and Sudden Income

For some young athletes, money arrives quickly.

NIL income, bonuses, or unexpected opportunities create risk if no structure exists. Without guidance, money is spent emotionally. Taxes are ignored. Saving is postponed.

In sports terms, this is a young player getting a contract before learning financial fundamentals.

Families should talk about:

- Separating spending and saving

- Planning for taxes
- Avoiding lifestyle inflation
- Building habits before building image

These conversations protect opportunity instead of limiting it.

## Aging Parents and Role Reversal

At some point, roles reverse.

Parents who once guided you may need help managing finances, healthcare, or logistics. These conversations are uncomfortable because they challenge identity, pride, and independence.

Avoiding them does not protect parents.

It leaves them exposed.

In football terms, this is leadership maturity.

Veterans step up. They communicate clearly. They protect the team even when conversations are hard.

Topics that eventually need discussion:

- Where documents are located
- Who has authority to help
- Healthcare preferences
- Financial accounts and bills
- Long-term care wishes

Waiting for a crisis makes everything harder.

## Why Proactive Conversations Matter With Parents

Most family crises are not caused by lack of love.

They are caused by lack of preparation.

When parents become ill or incapacitated, families scramble. Decisions are rushed. Emotions are high. Conflicts emerge because no one knows what was intended.

In sports terms, this is emergency substitution with no plan.

Preparation does not remove emotion, but it reduces chaos.

Approach these conversations with respect, humility, and empathy. This is not about taking control. It is about supporting independence for as long as possible.

## Family Expectations and Financial Boundaries

Boundaries protect relationships.

Helping family is not wrong. Supporting loved ones is often meaningful and necessary. The problem arises when help is unstructured, unspoken, or assumed.

In football terms, this is assignment clarity.

Undefined roles create conflict. Clear roles create trust.

Key boundary questions include:

- Is this a gift or a loan?
- What are expectations for repayment?
- How often will help occur?
- What happens if circumstances change?
- Who makes decisions?

Avoid vague arrangements.

Vagueness leads to resentment.

## Loans vs Gifts: Clarity Matters

Many family conflicts stem from money given without clear expectations.

One person thinks it is a loan. The other thinks it is a gift. Neither says it out loud. Resentment grows quietly.

In sports terms, this is miscommunication at the line of scrimmage.

Someone thought it was zone. Someone thought it was man. The result is a blown assignment.

Clarity upfront protects both sides.

If you choose to help, decide whether you are comfortable never getting the money back. If not, structure it clearly or do not do it.

## Money and Sibling Dynamics

Money conversations can amplify sibling dynamics.

Perceived favoritism. Unequal support. Different lifestyles. Old roles resurface quickly.

Parents should communicate intentions clearly. Adult siblings should avoid assumptions.

In football terms, this is locker room dynamics.

If players think treatment is unfair, chemistry suffers. Transparency matters.

Clear communication prevents misinterpretation.

## Why Silence Is the Most Expensive Strategy

Silence feels safe in the short term.

No conflict. No awkwardness. No emotion. Unfortunately, silence almost always creates bigger problems later.

In sports terms, this is ignoring film.

Mistakes do not fix themselves. They repeat until addressed.

Money conversations do not weaken families.

Avoiding them does.

## Coach's Perspective on Family Communication

A coach would say it plainly.

Communicate early.

Be clear.

Hold boundaries.

Protect the team.

Great teams talk through issues before they become problems. Families are no different.

Leadership includes communication.

## Game Situations and Decision Points

These moments define outcomes.

A family member needs help. Do you respond emotionally or with a plan?

Kids ask about money. Do you avoid the topic or teach intentionally?

Parents age. Do you prepare proactively or wait for crisis?

A boundary is crossed. Do you address it or stay silent?

Each decision compounds.

## Common Athlete Mistakes and Financial Parallels

Athletes avoid tough conversations.

Financially, that leads to confusion.

Athletes assume loyalty replaces structure.

Financially, that leads to resentment.

Athletes wait too long to address issues.

Financially, that leads to rushed decisions.

The pattern is familiar.

Avoidance delays discomfort. It increases damage.

## How to Start These Conversations

You do not need the perfect script.

You need willingness.

Start with curiosity, not accusation. Ask questions. Share goals. Express care. Set expectations calmly.

Examples:

- "I want to make sure we're aligned before we move forward."
- "I want to talk about this now so it doesn't become stressful later."
- "Can we clarify expectations so no one feels uncomfortable?"

Tone matters more than precision.

## Winning the Long Game

Families win together when communication is clear.

Money conversations done well build trust, confidence, and respect. They reduce conflict. They protect relationships. They allow support to happen without resentment.

Strong families do not avoid money.

They manage it openly.

## Athlete Takeaways

Money problems usually start with silence, not numbers.

Kids learn by watching behavior, not hearing lectures.

Early guidance prevents costly mistakes later.

College and young adults need coaching before problems show up.

Aging parents require proactive leadership.

Boundaries protect relationships.

Loans and gifts must be defined clearly.

Avoidance increases conflict. Communication prevents it.

In sports, communication keeps teams together.

In families, it does the same.

Talk early. Talk clearly. Protect the people who matter most.

# Part VI: Staying in the Game Long-Term

Every athlete knows the hardest part of competition is not getting ready.

It is staying ready.

Anyone can lock in for a week. Anyone can follow a plan when things are going well. The real test is what happens over time. After setbacks. After distractions. After success.

Staying in the game long-term is about habits, accountability, and perspective.

Money rewards those who keep showing up. Who keep doing the basics. Who avoid the mistakes that quietly end seasons early. Most financial failure does not come from one bad decision. It comes from drift. Complacency. Letting small issues go unaddressed.

This final part of the playbook is about leadership.

Knowing when to ask for help.

Knowing who to trust.

Knowing how to protect yourself from bad advice and scams.

Knowing how to learn from mistakes instead of repeating them.

Just like football, the game never gets easier. You just get better at playing it.

The athletes who win long after the whistle are not the ones who try to do everything themselves. They build a team. They stay disciplined. They respect the fundamentals.

This section ties everything together.

The goal is not perfection.

The goal is longevity.

If you can stay engaged, stay accountable, and stay disciplined, you give yourself a chance to win for decades.

That is how you stay in the game.

# Chapter 25: Advisors, Scams, and Winning Over the Long Haul

No championship team is built alone.

Even the best players rely on coaches, trainers, film staff, and teammates. Trying to do everything yourself is not toughness. It is ego. And ego shortens careers.

Money works the same way.

At some point, winning long-term requires support, perspective, and accountability.

## *When to Seek Professional Help*

You do not need an advisor for every decision. You need one when complexity increases.

Income grows.

Taxes become confusing.

Family responsibilities expand.

Investments feel overwhelming.

In football terms, this is calling in the coordinator. You still play the game. You just get better direction.

Asking for help is not weakness. It is professionalism.

## *Types of Financial Advisors*

Not all advisors are the same.

Some focus on investments only. Some focus on planning. Some sell products. Some act as fiduciaries.

In football terms, this is knowing whether you are talking to a head coach, a position coach, or a recruiter. Titles matter less than incentives.

Understand how advisors are paid. Know whose interests come first.

## *Recognizing Scams and Bad Advice*

Scams target athletes because visibility and income attract attention.

Guaranteed returns.

Urgency and pressure.

"Exclusive" opportunities.

Complex explanations that avoid clarity.

In football terms, this is trickery. If it sounds too good to be true, it probably is.

Bad advice is often confident and loud. Good advice is disciplined and boring.

## *Ten Common Financial Mistakes*

1. Spending before saving
2. Ignoring taxes
3. Carrying high-interest debt
4. Chasing hype
5. Skipping insurance
6. Overcomplicating investments
7. Panic selling
8. Ignoring beneficiaries
9. Waiting too long to start
10. Trusting the wrong people

These mistakes are preventable with structure and awareness.

## *Ten Rules for Long-Term Success*

1. Live below your means
2. Save automatically
3. Invest consistently
4. Protect what you earn
5. Avoid unnecessary debt
6. Keep it simple
7. Stay disciplined
8. Review, do not react
9. Ask for help when needed
10. Play the long game

## *Coach's Perspective*

A coach would say it clearly.
Build the right team.
Know who you trust.
Protect the locker room.
Stay disciplined.
Leadership means choosing the right help.

## *Game Situations and Decision Points*

You feel overwhelmed. Do you ask for help or avoid it?
You hear about an opportunity. Do you verify or rush?
You make a mistake. Do you learn or repeat it?
These choices define long-term outcomes.

## *Winning the Long Haul*

Winning with money is not about brilliance. It is about discipline, patience, and accountability.

Stay coachable.

Stay humble.

Stay consistent.

That is how you win long after the final whistle.

## *Athlete Takeaways*

- Professional help increases clarity, not dependence.
- Know how advisors are compensated.
- If it sounds too good to be true, it is.
- Mistakes are part of the process. Repeating them is not.
- Discipline wins over decades.

# Chapter 26: Losing the Schedule and Rebuilding Structure

The hardest part of football is not practice.

It is what happens when practice disappears.

When you are playing, your day is mapped out. Lifts are scheduled. Meetings are mandatory. Practice starts on time whether you feel ready or not. Structure is built into the environment.

Then the season ends. Or your career does.

Suddenly, no one is setting the calendar. No one is checking attendance. No one is holding you accountable for how you use your time. What once felt rigid is gone, and freedom takes its place.

That freedom is where many athletes struggle.

## *Why Life Gets Harder When No One Is Setting Your Calendar*

Structure creates momentum.

When your day is planned, decisions are reduced. You know where to be and when. Energy goes toward execution, not decision making.

When structure disappears, everything becomes optional.

Wake-up time.

Workouts.

Meal prep.

Spending discipline.

Saving.

Investing.

Optional sounds good until discipline fades.

In football terms, this is the difference between a scheduled practice and an open gym. One builds habits. The other depends on motivation.

Motivation is unreliable.

### *From Mandatory Workouts to Optional Discipline*

In football, discipline is enforced.

Miss a lift, there are consequences. Miss a meeting, there is accountability. The system does not care how you feel that day.

In life, discipline becomes optional. No one punishes you for skipping a workout. No one fines you for overspending. No one calls you out for ignoring your budget.

The absence of consequences creates drift.

Drift does not feel dangerous. It feels comfortable. And that is why it is so destructive.

### *How Lack of Structure Quietly Breaks Financial Habits*

Financial habits depend on repetition.

Saving regularly.

Paying bills on time.

Reviewing accounts.

Sticking to a plan during volatility.

Without structure, these habits weaken.

You mean to save later.

You plan to review statements next month.

You delay setting up automation.

Nothing breaks all at once. It erodes slowly.

In football terms, this is taking plays off. The damage does not show up immediately, but it shows up eventually.

## *Replacing Practice Schedules With Personal Systems*

Winning after football requires replacing external structure with internal systems.

You do not need motivation. You need routines.

Set fixed times for financial check-ins.

Automate savings and investing.

Create rules for spending and decision making.

Use calendars, reminders, and systems.

In football terms, this is building your own offseason program.

No coach is watching. The work still matters.

Systems protect you when motivation disappears. They create consistency when life gets busy. They keep you moving forward without relying on willpower.

## *Coach's Perspective*

A coach would say it plainly.

There are no off days.

Discipline equals freedom.

How you practice is how you play.

Nobody is coming to save you.

Structure is not restriction. It is protection.

## *Game Situations and Decision Points*

You have flexibility now. Do you create routines or drift?

No one checks your spending. Do you build rules or rely on feel?

You feel busy but unfocused. Do you rebuild structure or blame circumstances?

These decisions shape everything else.

## *Common Athlete Mistakes and Financial Parallels*

Athletes rely on motivation.

Financially, that leads to inconsistency.

Athletes resist structure after sports.

Financially, that leads to drift.

Athletes confuse freedom with lack of discipline.

Financially, that leads to regret.

## *Winning the Long Game*

Football gave you structure. Life requires you to build it.

The athletes who win long after the whistle are not the most talented. They are the most disciplined. They replace team schedules with personal systems and keep showing up when no one is watching.

Structure is how you stay sharp.

Systems are how you stay consistent.

That is how you keep winning without a coach setting the clock.

## *Athlete Takeaways*

- Freedom without structure leads to drift.
- Discipline must replace mandatory schedules.
- Financial habits depend on repetition.
- Systems beat motivation every time.
- Build your own structure and protect it.

# Chapter 27: From Teammates to Coworkers

Think about your first real team meeting.

Everyone knew the rules. There was a head coach. Position coaches. Clear authority. Clear roles. Clear consequences. If you messed up, the film showed it. If you played well, it showed that too.

Now think about your first job after sports.

No depth chart.

No film.

No clear scoreboard.

Just meetings, emails, and expectations that seem to change depending on who you talk to.

That shift catches a lot of former athletes off guard.

## *Why the Workplace Feels Foreign After Sports*

Sports environments are built on clarity.

You know who is in charge.

You know what winning looks like.

You know how performance is measured.

Workplaces are different.

Success is often subjective. Authority is layered. Feedback is indirect. Performance reviews happen once or twice a year instead of after every game.

For athletes used to immediate accountability, this can feel disorienting.

In football terms, it is like playing a game where the rules are not fully explained and the scoreboard is hidden.

### *Authority Without Coaches*

In sports, authority is obvious.

Coaches set the plan. They correct mistakes. They decide playing time.

In the workplace, authority is more subtle.

Managers may not coach. Leaders may avoid conflict. Decisions may be influenced by relationships rather than performance alone.

Former athletes often expect coaching that never comes. They wait to be corrected instead of seeking clarity.

That hesitation can stall growth.

### *Feedback Without Film*

Film does not lie.

You either made the play or you did not.

Workplaces rarely work that way.

Feedback may be delayed, softened, or avoided entirely. You might not know you are off track until it shows up in a performance review, a missed promotion, or a job change.

Athletes used to instant correction can misread silence as approval.

In football terms, this is not checking the film and assuming everything went fine.

### *Politics, Ambiguity, and Unclear Expectations*

This is one of the biggest adjustments.

Workplaces involve personalities, incentives, and unspoken rules. People may protect their roles. Credit may not be evenly distributed. Expectations may shift without notice.

None of this feels fair to athletes raised in merit-based systems.

But ignoring it does not make it go away.

Understanding the environment helps you navigate it without compromising integrity.

## *How This Impacts Income Growth and Career Stability*

Career growth is tied to clarity.

If you do not understand how success is measured, you cannot optimize for it. If you do not seek feedback, you may plateau. If you assume effort alone is enough, income growth can stall.

In football terms, this is working hard in the wrong scheme.

The most successful former athletes learn to translate their discipline into proactive communication. They ask questions. They seek feedback. They learn how decisions are made.

That awareness directly affects promotions, raises, and long-term stability.

## *Coach's Perspective*

A coach would frame it like this.

Do not assume.

Ask questions.

Learn the system.

Control what you can control.

Different field. Same fundamentals.

## *Game Situations and Decision Points*

You are unsure how performance is evaluated. Do you ask or guess?

You receive vague feedback. Do you press for clarity or stay quiet?

You feel overlooked. Do you adjust strategy or disengage?

These moments determine career trajectory.

## *Common Athlete Mistakes and Financial Parallels*

Athletes wait for coaching.

Career-wise, that delays growth.

Athletes rely on effort alone.

Career-wise, that ignores visibility and alignment.

Athletes avoid politics entirely.

Career-wise, that limits influence.

## *Winning the Long Game*

The workplace is not the locker room. But the same traits still matter.

Discipline. Preparation. Accountability. Coachability.

The difference is that now, you must seek structure instead of having it handed to you.

When you learn the system, you stop feeling lost. When you understand expectations, income growth follows.

## *Athlete Takeaways*

- Workplaces operate without clear scoreboards.
- Authority and feedback are less direct than sports.
- Silence is not the same as approval.
- Clarity drives career growth and income stability.
- Learn the system and play it with discipline.

# Chapter 28: When No One Is Watching Anymore

Some of the hardest workouts were never televised.

Early mornings. Empty weight rooms. Offseason lifts when the season felt far away. No crowd. No cameras. No applause. Just you, the work, and the standard.

Those moments built everything.

Then football ends.

And for the first time in your life, no one is watching anymore.

No coach checking attendance.

No teammate pushing pace.

No consequence for taking today off.

That is where the real test begins.

## *The Discipline Gap After Accountability Disappears*

In sports, discipline is enforced.

Miss a rep, there is a consequence. Miss a meeting, it is addressed. Accountability is built into the environment.

After sports, accountability becomes optional.

You can skip the gym.

You can ignore your budget.

You can delay saving.

You can avoid uncomfortable decisions.

Nothing happens immediately.

That delay creates a discipline gap. Not because former athletes are lazy, but because the system that enforced discipline is gone.

## *Why Former Athletes Self-Sabotage Without Pressure*

Pressure keeps standards high.

When pressure disappears, comfort sneaks in.

Former athletes are used to external pressure driving behavior. When it is gone, many unconsciously recreate pressure in unhealthy ways. Overspending. Risky decisions. Chasing excitement. Creating chaos.

It is not weakness. It is misdirected energy.

In football terms, this is playing sloppy when the game feels meaningless. Standards slip without immediate consequences.

## *Comfort vs Growth Decisions*

After sports, comfort becomes tempting.

Sleep in.

Spend freely.

Avoid hard conversations.

Delay long-term planning.

Comfort feels earned. Growth feels optional.

But growth always requires discomfort.

In football terms, this is choosing recovery over conditioning every day. It feels good now. It costs you later.

Money decisions follow the same pattern. Comfort spending today often creates financial pressure tomorrow.

## *Translating "Grind Culture" Into Adult Life*

Grind culture worked in sports because it was structured.

Lift here.

Practice there.

Meetings at this time.

After sports, grinding without structure leads to burnout.

Adult discipline is quieter.

Consistency over intensity.

Systems over willpower.

Planning over reacting.

Grinding now means showing up for boring reps. Reviewing finances. Saving automatically. Investing consistently. Having uncomfortable conversations.

It is not loud. It is effective.

## *Why Money Mistakes Show Up Years Later*

Money is delayed feedback.

You can overspend for years before consequences show up. You can avoid investing and still feel fine. You can ignore insurance and never need it. Until you do.

In football, mistakes are immediate. In money, they compound quietly.

By the time problems appear, the behavior that caused them is long forgotten.

That is why discipline matters most when nothing seems wrong.

## *Coach's Perspective*

A coach would not soften this.

Standards do not disappear because no one is watching.

Do not confuse comfort with success.

Discipline is who you are, not who is checking.

Champions work in silence.

The work still counts.

## *Game Situations and Decision Points*

You have flexibility now. Do you drift or build structure?

You feel comfortable financially. Do you prepare or coast?

No one checks your habits. Do you raise or lower your standards?

These decisions compound quietly.

## *Common Athlete Mistakes and Financial Parallels*

Athletes rely on pressure.

Financially, that leads to drift without it.

Athletes chase comfort after sacrifice.

Financially, that leads to overspending.

Athletes grind without structure.

Financially, that leads to burnout or chaos.

## *Winning the Long Game*

The most important reps happen when no one is watching.

That is true in football.

That is true in money.

That is true in life.

If you can build discipline without an audience, you will outperform people with more talent, more income, and more opportunity.

Standards matter even when the lights are off.

### *Athlete Takeaways*

- Accountability disappears. Discipline must remain.
- Comfort today creates pressure tomorrow.
- Grind culture must evolve into systems.
- Money punishes mistakes slowly, then all at once.
- Champions work when no one is watching.

# Chapter 29: Redefining Winning After the Uniform Comes Off

Every player knows exactly how winning is measured on the field.

Scoreboard.

Film.

Stats.

Wins and losses.

There is no debate. You either performed or you did not. Preparation shows up on tape. Mistakes are visible. Results are clear.

Then football ends.

And suddenly, the scoreboard disappears.

No points. No rankings. No depth chart. Just a vague sense that you are supposed to be "doing well" without anyone ever defining what that actually means. No weekly opponent. No final whistle. No coach explaining whether you are ahead or behind.

That is where a lot of former athletes get lost.

## *Why Chasing Status Replaces Chasing Performance*

In sports, performance is the currency.

You earn respect through preparation, execution, and results. Status follows performance, not the other way around. Playing time, leadership, and recognition all come from doing the work and producing on the field.

After sports, the order often flips.

Status starts to replace performance.

Job titles.

Income levels.

Cars.

Houses.

Social media highlights.

Without a clear scoreboard, it is easy to borrow one from society. The problem is that borrowed scoreboards reward appearance, not substance. They measure what is visible, not what is sustainable.

Former athletes who once chased performance begin chasing validation. And validation is a moving target. No matter how much you accumulate, someone always appears ahead. The finish line keeps moving because it was never clearly defined in the first place.

## *Income vs Fulfillment*

Income matters.

It provides stability. It creates options. It reduces stress. Pretending otherwise is dishonest. Money solves real problems.

But income alone does not equal winning.

Many former athletes reach income milestones and still feel unsettled. The drive is there, but the purpose is not. They did what they thought they were supposed to do. They followed the path that looked successful. And yet something feels off.

In football terms, this is piling up yards without scoring.

You are moving. You are working. You are busy. But the result does not feel like winning.

Fulfillment comes from alignment. Using your skills. Building something meaningful. Having control over your time and decisions. Feeling progress without constant pressure.

Money supports fulfillment. It does not create it.

### *Titles, Houses, Cars, and Comparison Traps*

Comparison never ends.

Someone is always making more. Someone has a bigger house. Someone has a better title. Someone looks happier online. There is no off-season from comparison if you let it run unchecked.

Former athletes are especially vulnerable because competition is wired into who you are. You were trained to measure yourself against others. The difference is that sports had rules. Adult life does not.

Comparing yourself without a defined standard is like playing a game without boundaries. You never feel finished. There is always another metric, another benchmark, another person to chase.

Status purchases often fill that gap temporarily. A new car. A bigger house. A better title. The feeling lasts for a moment. Then it fades. Then the chase starts again.

That cycle is exhausting.

### *What Success Actually Looks Like in Your 30s and 40s*

Success changes as life evolves.

In your 30s and 40s, winning often looks different than it did in your early twenties. It looks quieter. Less visible. More intentional.

Winning starts to look like:

Consistency instead of chaos.

Freedom instead of flash.

Health instead of burnout.

Time with family instead of constant pressure.

Confidence instead of comparison.

There may be fewer highlights, but there is more control. Fewer people watching, but more peace. Less noise, but more clarity.

The mistake is using a young athlete's scoreboard to judge an adult life. That scoreboard was built for a different season.

Different season. Different rules.

## *Building a New Scoreboard*

If you do not define winning, you will always chase it.

You need a new scoreboard. Not society's. Yours.

That scoreboard might include:

Financial stability without constant stress.

Work that aligns with your values.

Flexibility in your schedule.

Progress toward long-term goals.

Peace of mind.

These are measurable if you choose to measure them. They just do not show up on a highlight reel.

In football terms, this is defining what winning the season actually means. Is it championships only, or is it health, development, and longevity? Great programs know the answer before the season starts.

When you build your own scoreboard, decisions get easier. Spending aligns. Career choices make sense. Comparison loses power. You stop reacting to noise and start choosing intentionally.

## *Coach's Perspective*

A coach would say it straight.

Define the standard.

Do not chase noise.

Know what winning looks like for you.

Play your game.

Undefined goals lead to wasted effort. Clear standards focus energy.

## *Game Situations and Decision Points*

This shows up in everyday moments.

You get a promotion. Does it align with your life, or just look good?

You feel behind. Are you measuring against the right scoreboard?

You want more. Is it growth you want, or validation?

These questions shape the next decade more than any single decision.

## *Common Athlete Mistakes and Financial Parallels*

Athletes chase recognition.

Financially, that leads to status spending.

Athletes use old metrics.

Financially, that leads to misaligned goals.

Athletes compete without boundaries.

Financially, that leads to burnout.

The pattern is familiar. Intensity without direction eventually breaks down.

## *Winning the Long Game*

Winning after football is not about proving anything.

It is about building a life that works. A life that supports your values, relationships, health, and future. A life where money is a tool, not a measuring stick.

When you stop chasing someone else's scoreboard and start tracking what actually matters, the pressure eases. Decisions feel intentional. Progress feels real.

That is real success.

## *Athlete Takeaways*

- Status is not the same as performance
- Income supports fulfillment but does not define it
- Comparison traps never end unless you step out
- Success changes with seasons of life
- Borrowed scoreboards reward appearance, not substance

You trained your whole life to win by the rules of the game.
Now it is your turn to define the rules that matter most.

# Chapter 30: Staying Connected Without Living in the Past

The locker room was never just a room.

It was where you belonged. Where inside jokes lived. Where accountability was shared. Where someone noticed when you were off and called you out. Where wins were celebrated and losses were processed together. It was a space with standards, rhythm, and shared purpose.

Then one day, it is gone.

No group chat.

No daily check-ins.

No shared mission.

For many former athletes, that loss hits harder than they expect. Not because they miss drills or conditioning, but because they miss connection. They miss being known. They miss being part of something bigger than themselves.

## *The Role of Community, Mentorship, and New Locker Rooms*

Teams do more than train bodies. They create identity.

When the team disappears, identity often feels fragmented. You are still disciplined. Still driven. Still capable. But without a place to direct those traits, they can feel untethered. That is why community matters so much after sports. Not as a replacement for the past, but as a bridge to the future.

New locker rooms look different.

Workplaces.

Entrepreneur groups.

Faith communities.

Mentorship circles.

Former athlete networks.

They do not have uniforms or practice schedules, but they serve the same function. Shared standards. Mutual accountability. Support. Perspective. Challenge.

You do not stop needing teammates when sports end. You just need different ones.

## *Why Isolation Hits Former Athletes Hard*

Athletes are rarely alone.

There is always someone around. Teammates in the locker room. Coaches in meetings. Staff on the sidelines. Even quiet moments are shared. Isolation is unfamiliar.

After sports, isolation creeps in quietly. Schedules no longer overlap. Friends move on to different seasons of life. Competition becomes individual. No one checks in unless something is obviously wrong.

That lack of connection weakens more than mood. It weakens discipline.

Without people, standards slip. Motivation fades. Structure erodes. Not because you do not care, but because discipline without connection eventually loses meaning.

Connection keeps you sharp.

Connection keeps you accountable.

Connection reminds you why effort matters.

## *Finding Purpose Without the Team*

Purpose in sports is built in.

Practice. Compete. Win. Repeat.

After sports, purpose must be chosen. That can feel uncomfortable for athletes used to assigned roles and clear expectations. But it is also an opportunity most people never get.

Purpose after sports can come from building something meaningful. Teaching others. Leading teams. Serving communities. Creating value. Raising families. Mentoring younger athletes. Contributing beyond yourself.

Money plays a role here.

When money is aligned with purpose, it becomes a tool. It funds freedom, impact, and growth. When purpose is missing, money becomes empty. Chasing income without meaning feels hollow, no matter how much you earn.

Purpose gives direction to discipline.

## *Healthy Nostalgia vs Being Stuck*

Remembering your playing days is healthy.

They shaped you. They mattered. They taught lessons that still apply.

Living there is not healthy.

Healthy nostalgia honors the past without letting it define the present. Being stuck means measuring everything against what used to be and finding today lacking.

In sports terms, this is the difference between watching film to learn and watching film to relive.

One helps you improve.

The other keeps you frozen.

Your past matters. It is not your future.

## *Creating a Forward-Looking Identity*

Identity after sports is not found. It is built.

Built through choices.

Built through consistency.

Built through contribution.

Former athletes who thrive do not cling to titles. They carry values forward. Discipline. Leadership. Accountability. Teamwork. Resilience. Those traits are portable. They work in business, family, community, and service.

When identity moves forward, connection becomes natural again. You gravitate toward people who share standards. You seek environments that challenge you. You create new locker rooms without forcing it.

## *Mentorship as a Two-Way Street*

Mentorship matters more after sports than many athletes realize.

Having mentors provides perspective and guidance during transition. Being a mentor provides purpose and grounding. Both roles reinforce identity and connection.

In the locker room, veterans teach rookies without being asked. That dynamic does not disappear after sports. It just needs a new setting.

Teaching what you have learned helps you move forward without forgetting where you came from.

## *Coach's Perspective*

A coach would say it clearly.

Honor the past.

Do not live in it.

Find your next team.

Lead where you are.

Growth requires movement. Standing still feels safe, but it keeps you disconnected.

## *Game Situations and Decision Points*

These moments shape the next chapter.

You miss the locker room. Do you isolate or seek community?

You feel disconnected. Do you reach out or withdraw?

You feel stuck. Do you build forward or relive backward?

These choices feel small. They are not. They determine whether identity expands or contracts.

## *Common Athlete Mistakes and Financial Parallels*

Athletes isolate after sports.

Emotionally, that weakens discipline and purpose.

Athletes cling to old identity.

Financially, that leads to chasing status instead of alignment.

Athletes avoid new communities.

Personally, that limits growth and opportunity.

The pattern is familiar. Avoidance delays discomfort. It deepens it.

## *Winning the Long Game*

You do not move forward by cutting off the past. You move forward by building on it.

Connection matters. Community matters. Purpose matters.

When you find new locker rooms, discipline strengthens. Decisions align. Money becomes supportive instead of stressful. Life feels lighter because you are not carrying it alone.

You were never meant to do this by yourself.

## *Athlete Takeaways*

- The locker room mattered because connection mattered
- Losing community after sports is real and impactful
- Isolation weakens discipline, motivation, and purpose
- You still need teammates, just in new forms
- Purpose must be chosen after sports, not assigned

You belonged once for a reason.

Find places where you belong again.

# Glossary of Football and Financial Terms

This glossary translates common football language into financial meaning and explains key money terms using concepts athletes already understand. Use it as a quick reference when something feels unfamiliar or needs a reset.

## *A*

**Asset**

Something you own that has value. Cash, investments, property, or a business.

*Football parallel:* Talent on the roster.

**Asset Allocation**

How you divide money among stocks, bonds, and cash.

*Football parallel:* Building the right lineup.

## *B*

**Bond**

A loan you make to a company or government that pays interest.

*Football parallel:* Playing defense and controlling the clock.

**Budget**

A plan for how money comes in and goes out.

*Football parallel:* Weekly game plan.

## C

**Cash Flow**

Money coming in minus money going out.

*Football parallel:* Yards gained versus yards allowed.

**Compounding**

Earning returns on top of previous returns over time.

*Football parallel:* Stacking good days and consistent reps.

**Credit Score**

A measure of how reliably you handle borrowed money.

*Football parallel:* Trust level with the coaching staff.

## D

**Debt**

Money you owe to someone else.

*Football parallel:* Playing with borrowed field position.

**Diversification**

Spreading investments to reduce risk.

*Football parallel:* Roster depth.

**Dividend**

Cash paid to shareholders from company profits.

*Football parallel:* Points scored while the clock keeps running.

## E

**Emergency Fund**

Cash set aside for unexpected expenses.

*Football parallel:* Injury insurance.

**ETF (Exchange-Traded Fund)**

A basket of investments that trades like a stock.

*Football parallel:* Team-based execution.

**Expense Ratio**

Annual cost of running a fund.
*Football parallel:* Penalties that quietly add up.

## *F*

**Fees**
Costs charged for managing or trading investments.
*Football parallel:* Giving up free yards.
**Fixed Expense**
A cost that stays mostly the same.
*Football parallel:* Base defense.

## G

**Growth Investing**
Focusing on companies expected to grow faster than average.
*Football parallel:* Speed and explosiveness.

## *H*

**Herd Mentality**
Following the crowd instead of the plan.
*Football parallel:* Letting crowd noise dictate play-calling.

## *I*

**Index Fund**
A fund designed to match market performance.
*Football parallel:* Running the base offense.
**Inflation**
Rising prices over time that reduce purchasing power.
*Football parallel:* Playing uphill football.
**Insurance**

Protection against major financial loss.

*Football parallel:* Pads and protective gear.

## L

**Liability**

Money you owe.

*Football parallel:* Vulnerabilities on defense.

**Liquidity**

How quickly you can access cash.

*Football parallel:* Field position flexibility.

## M

**Market Volatility**

Normal ups and downs in investment prices.

*Football parallel:* Momentum swings.

**Mutual Fund**

A pooled investment managed by professionals.

*Football parallel:* Structured practice plan.

## N

**Net Worth**

Assets minus liabilities.

*Football parallel:* Overall matchup strength.

## O

**Opportunity Cost**

What you give up when choosing one option over another.

*Football parallel:* Missed assignment elsewhere on the field.

## *P*

**Premium**

Cost to keep insurance active.

*Football parallel:* Staying game-ready.

**Portfolio**

All of your investments combined.

*Football parallel:* Full roster.

## *R*

**Rebalancing**

Adjusting investments back to target allocation.

*Football parallel:* Halftime adjustments.

**Risk Tolerance**

How much uncertainty you feel comfortable with.

*Football parallel:* Confidence under pressure.

**Risk Capacity**

How much risk you can actually afford to take.

*Football parallel:* Depth and durability.

## *S*

**Savings Account**

A place to store cash safely.

*Football parallel:* Sideline protection.

**Stock**

Ownership in a company.

*Football parallel:* Being part of the organization.

## *T*

**Tax-Advantaged Account**

An account with tax benefits.

*Football parallel:* Knowing the rulebook.

**Total Return**

Investment growth plus income received.

*Football parallel:* Full scoreboard, not just touchdowns.

## *V*

**Variable Expense**

A cost that changes month to month.

*Football parallel:* Play-calling flexibility.

## *W*

**Will**

Legal document directing what happens to assets after death.

*Football parallel:* Emergency playbook.

This glossary is not about memorizing terms. It is about understanding the language of money the same way you learned the language of football. When the terms make sense, the game slows down.

# Disclaimers

## Educational Purposes Only

This book is for educational purposes only.

The information provided in *Football Money 101* is intended to help readers understand general financial concepts using cheer-based analogies. It does not provide individualized financial, investment, tax, legal, or insurance advice.

Every financial situation is different. Your goals, income, family circumstances, risk tolerance, and time horizon are unique. What works for one person may not be appropriate for another.

## Not Financial, Investment, or Legal Advice

Nothing in this book should be interpreted as a recommendation to buy, sell, or hold any specific investment, financial product, or strategy.

This book does not replace advice from qualified professionals, including:

### Financial advisors

### Accountants or tax professionals

### Attorneys

## Insurance professionals

Before making financial decisions, readers should consult professionals who can evaluate their individual circumstances.

## No Guarantees or Promises of Results

All investing involves risk, including the possible loss of principal.

Past performance does not guarantee future results. Markets fluctuate. Economic conditions change. Outcomes cannot be predicted or guaranteed.

Examples and scenarios in this book are illustrative only and may not reflect actual results or real-world outcomes.

## Tax and Legal Information

Any discussion of taxes, retirement accounts, estate planning, or legal structures is general in nature.

Tax laws and regulations change frequently and vary by jurisdiction. Legal requirements differ based on location and personal circumstances.

Readers should seek personalized tax or legal advice before acting on any information related to these topics.

## Athlete and Career Considerations

This book discusses financial topics as they relate to athletes and former athletes, including career transitions and income changes.

It does not provide career placement services, employment advice, or guarantees related to income, compensation, or career success.

## Use of Analogies

Cheer and sports analogies are used to make financial concepts easier to understand.

These analogies are educational tools only and should not be interpreted literally. Financial decisions require analysis beyond analogy.

## Personal Responsibility

By reading this book, you acknowledge that:

### You are responsible for your own financial decisions

### You understand that financial outcomes involve uncertainty

### You agree to seek appropriate professional guidance when needed

Education improves decision-making, but responsibility remains with the individual.

## Contact Information

If you would like to learn more about the concepts discussed in this book or explore additional educational resources, Pat Brown can be found through public platforms including LinkedIn, Twitter, or via a Google search.

For questions specifically related to Football *Money 101,* you may contact Pat Brown at:

**info@footballmoney101.com**

## Final Reminder

Financial success is built over time through discipline, planning, and consistency.

This book provides a framework, not a guarantee.

Use it as a guide, not a substitute for professional advice.

Pat Brown OLB, University of Kansas

Made in the USA
Monee, IL
04 November 2026

67376087R00134